PAGES FROM HISTORY

World War II

A HISTORY IN DOCUMENTS

World War II
A HISTORY IN DOCUMENTS

James H. Madison

New York   Oxford
OXFORD UNIVERSITY PRESS
2010

Dedicated to my students at Indiana University, who taught me so much about the past and the present.

General Editors

Sarah Deutsch
Professor of History
Duke University

Carol K. Karlsen
Professor of History
University of Michigan

Robert G. Moeller
Professor of History
University of California, Irvine

Jeffrey N. Wasserstrom
Professor of History
University of California, Irvine

Cover: British soldiers take cover from sniper fire in a Dutch town.

Frontispiece: Adolf Hitler in front of the Eiffel Tower, Paris, June 23, 1940.

Title page: Flight deck of the USS *Bunker Hill* after it was hit by kamikazes near Okinawa, May 11, 1945.

Oxford University Press, Inc., publishes works that further Oxford University's objective of excellence in research, scholarship, and education.

Oxford New York
Auckland   Cape Town   Dar es Salaam   Hong Kong   Karachi
Kuala Lumpur   Madrid   Melbourne   Mexico City   Nairobi
New Delhi   Shanghai   Taipei   Toronto

With offices in
Argentina   Austria   Brazil   Chile   Czech Republic   France   Greece
Guatemala   Hungary   Italy   Japan   Poland   Portugal   Singapore
South Korea   Switzerland   Thailand   Turkey   Ukraine   Vietnam

Copyright © 2010 by Oxford University Press, Inc.

Published by Oxford University Press, Inc.

198 Madison Avenue, New York, New York 10016
http://www.oup.com

Oxford is a registered trademark of Oxford University Press

Library of Congress Cataloging-in-Publication Data
Madison, James H.
  World War II : a history in documents / [compiled by] James H. Madison.
    p. cm.
  Summary: "The documents in this book point readers to the major themes and issues of World War II, including major causes, course, and consequences of the war. Coverage is worldwide, with attention to home front as well as battlefront issues. Diplomacy and strategy blend with insights into the lives of ordinary people around the world"—Provided by publisher.
  Includes bibliographical references and index.
  ISBN 978-0-19-533812-6 (paper : alk. paper) — ISBN 978-0-19-516176-2 (cloth : alk. paper) 1. World War, 1939-1945—Sources. I. Title.
  D735.M336 2009
  940.53—dc22

                                                                    2009000576

Contents

What is a Document?

To the historian, a document is, quite simply, any sort of historical evidence. It is a primary source, the raw material of history. A document may be more than the expected government paperwork, such as a treaty or passport. It is also a letter, diary, will, grocery list, newspaper article, recipe, memoir, oral history, school yearbook, map, chart, architectural plan, poster, musical score, play script, novel, political cartoon, painting, photograph—even an object.

Using primary sources allows us not just to read *about* history, but to read history itself. It allows us to immerse ourselves in the look and feel of an era gone by, to understand its people and their language, whether verbal or visual. And it allows us to take an active, hands-on role in (re)constructing history.

Using primary sources requires us to use our powers of detection to ferret out the relevant facts and to draw conclusions from them; just as Agatha Christie uses the scores in a bridge game to determine the identity of a murderer, the historian uses facts from a variety of sources—some, perhaps, seemingly inconsequential—to build a historical case.

The poet W. H. Auden wrote that history was the study of questions. Primary sources force us to ask questions—and then, by answering them, to construct a narrative or an argument that makes sense to us. Moreover, as we draw on the many sources from "the dust-bin of history," we can endow that narrative with character, personality, and texture—all the elements that make history so endlessly intriguing.

Cartoon

This political cartoon addresses the issue of church and state. It illustrates the Supreme Court's role in balancing the demands of the 1st Amendment of the Constitution and the desires of the religious population.

Illustration

Illustrations from children's books, such as this alphabet from the *New England Primer*, tell us how children were educated, and also what the religious and moral values of the time were.

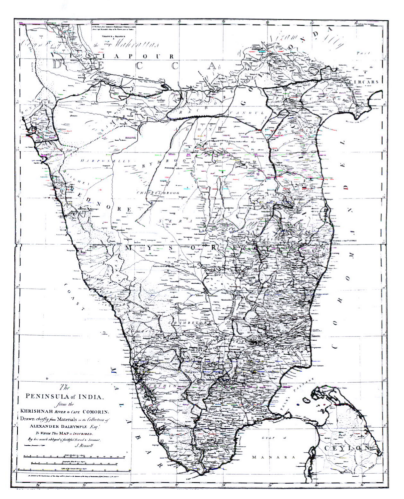

Treaty

A government document such as this 1805 treaty can reveal not only the details of government policy, but information about the people who signed it. Here, the Indians' names were written in English transliteration by U.S. officials, the Indians added pictographs to the right of their names.

Map

A 1788 British map of India shows the region prior to British colonization, an indication of the kingdoms and provinces whose ethnic divisions would resurface later in India's history.

Object

In this fifteenth-century ewer, both the physical materials of brass and silver and the iconic depiction of heaven as a forest display the refinement of the owner, an Egyptian sultan's wife. Objects, along with manuscripts and printed materials, provide evidence about the past.

How to Read a Document

When put in historical contexts, letters, speeches, photographs, poems, diaries, posters, and songs help us to imagine what it was like to live in a particular time and place, to understand the issues and controversies, to think about how that past might be both similar to and very different from our own time.

Documents require thoughtful and careful reading that compares, questions, and analyzes. Who produced the document? Who was the intended audience? What does the document say or show, exactly, down to the small details? What is missing? What does the document maker want us to *not* know and *not* think about?

Because war is so contentious and troubling, especially World War II, the documents in this book are likely to elicit anger or sadness as well as joy and gratitude. Strong emotional responses may be appropriate, but these primary sources also demand thoughtful, deliberate analysis.

The images and texts reproduced here come from all over the world and from great leaders and ordinary people. They ask that we try to imagine what life was like for people of different nations, races, ages, ideologies, and classes. A Japanese teenager and a German schoolgirl, for example, may have had some similar feelings about war, but they likely also had very different experiences.

The two documents on the opposite page illustrate some of the many voices that primary sources bring to us today. A photograph and a speech may look simple at first glance, but a closer look sparks insights that deepen and widen our understanding.

Subject

The photograph was taken June 14, 1940, as victorious German soldiers marched down a Paris street. The Nazi invaders had made swift progress into France, and after six short weeks forced a humiliating surrender that few French citizens had anticipated.

Interpretation

The photograph shows no marching Germans soldiers; rather, we see only French citizens standing on the sidewalk observing. Our eye catches first the weeping man. He is well-dressed, standing erect, but unable to hold back his tears. And then we move to the others, each with different expressions that show intense responses to the reality of defeat. A German citizen in 1940 would likely have viewed this photograph as exhilarating evidence of a great triumph. For most French people the photograph was, and remains, evidence of their darkest hour.

Text

This is the first page of one the most famous presidential speeches in American history. Speaking to Congress on December 8, 1941, the day after Japan attacked Pearl Harbor, President Franklin D. Roosevelt asked for a declaration of war. Congress quickly consented, and that same day the United States went to war.

Interpretation

President Roosevelt made his own handwritten revisions on this copy of the typed speech. Thinking carefully about his audience, which included the American people listening on the radio as well as Congress, the president made clear that Japan was the aggressor nation, evidenced, for example, in his use of the passive voice. He added dashes to remind himself to pause at a particular place. And he changed several words. Perhaps most importantly, he deleted "world history" and inserted "infamy," a word that carried much stronger meaning. FDR's speech is often referred to as the "Infamy Speech." Americans throughout the war years would remember the day and the date, December 7, in part because they would remember hearing the president's speech.

DRAFT No. 1   December 7, 1941.

PROPOSED MESSAGE TO THE CONGRESS

Yesterday, December 7, 1941, a date which will live in ~~world history~~ infamy,
the United States of America was ~~simultaneously~~ suddenly and deliberately attacked
by naval and air forces of the Empire of Japan. ~~without warning~~

The United States was at the moment at peace with that nation and was
still in ~~continuing the~~ conversation with its Government and its Emperor looking
toward the maintenance of peace in the Pacific. Indeed, one hour after,
Japanese air squadrons had commenced bombing in Oahu ~~Hawaii and the Philippines~~,
the Japanese Ambassador to the United States and his colleague delivered
to the Secretary of State a formal reply to a recent American ~~former~~ message. ~~from the~~
~~Secretary.~~ While This reply ~~contained a statement~~ stated that diplomatic negotiations
~~must be considered at an end,~~ it contained no threat ~~and no~~ or hint of ~~an~~ war or
armed attack.

It will be recorded that the distance ~~of Honolulu, and especially~~ of
Hawaii, from Japan makes it obvious that the attack was ~~were~~ deliberately
planned many days or even weeks ago. During the intervening time the Japanese Government has deliberately sought to deceive the United States by false
statements and expressions of hope for continued peace.

Introduction

In a public opinion poll at the end of the twentieth century, Americans ranked World War II as the most important event of the century. Many people elsewhere in the world agreed. This was the largest, most destructive war in human history. It changed the course of history, and its effects remain into the twenty-first century in all nations and among all peoples.

World War II was a total war. It demanded that all the resources of each nation focus on victory. This meant that millions of men and large numbers of women went into military uniform. It meant that civilians on the home fronts turned from their own families and private needs to the demands of war. It meant that governments assumed unprecedented power to direct the war effort, power that even in the democratic nations took away some cherished freedoms. The necessities of this total war demanded much of everyone.

World War II was a brutal war, the most brutal in human history. Americans especially like to remember it as a "good war." But that myth stalls in the face of the war's horrible death and destruction. Between fifty and sixty million people died, so many in such horrendous ways that historians will never know the exact number. While millions died fighting, the majority of the dead were civilians. The death and suffering increased as the war proceeded, fed by new weapons, new hatreds, new reasons for revenge against the enemy. Nations sent their airplanes to drop bombs on cities, on Shanghai,

This large crater made by a German bomb swallows a double-decker London bus in October 1940. German air raids over England between August 1940 and May 1941 caused the deaths of more than 40,000 civilians.

Rotterdam, London, Coventry, Hamburg, Berlin, Tokyo, and, finally, Hiroshima and Nagasaki. Killing people in these cities, as well as destroying factories and railroad yards, became a necessity of war, or so each side concluded.

This was a war made more horrible by notions of racial and national superiority. The Nazis set out to build an empire that would endure for a thousand years, a "Reich" founded on the superiority of the so-called Aryan people. Those who did not fit Nazi racial definitions were relegated to servitude and often to death. The Germans who created the Holocaust killed approximately six million Jews and also Slavs, homosexuals, the disabled, and other people deemed unfit to live. In Asia the Japanese claimed to be the nation of the rising sun, a people descended from the sun goddess and superior to all others. They applied this arrogance in brutal warfare against the Chinese, Korean, Filipino, and other peoples of Asia. All nations had some of these sorts of ideas about race and national superiority, though few others carried them so far. American GIs fighting against the Japanese, for example, tended toward more brutality against these "yellow" people than toward "white" German or Italian enemies. America's ideals of equality did not even apply to all Americans, particularly not to African Americans, who fought under the stars and stripes in mostly segregated military units.

The Axis nations—principally Germany, Japan, and Italy—were the aggressor nations, eager to go to war in the 1930s. The peace settlement at the end of World War I had left them bitter and convinced they deserved more territory, more military and economic strength, and more influence as great nations. The Allied nations—chiefly Britain, the United States, and the Soviet Union—were reluctant to fight. World War I had left their citizens fearfully mindful of the high costs of going to war. Fighting the great economic depression of the 1930s seemed more important. Many, especially Americans, argued for pacifism or noninvolvement in the affairs of others. They would fight only after it became clear that there was no alternative. By then, however, the Axis had a head start, so that in the first years they achieved impressive victories in Asia and Europe. They might have won. It is too easy to forget that Allied victory was not inevitable, to forget that those engaged in this war in 1941 or 1942 did not know what we know today.

It's hard to imagine the darkness that would have enveloped the world had the Axis nations won. These were fascist nations that dismissed democracy, focused attention on a great leader (Adolf Hitler, Mussolini, Emperor Hirohito), built their military strength, and were determined to expand their territories and to conquer and rule other people. These nations began a war the Allies had to win if the world was to have any hope of peace and of liberty and justice for all people. For the Allies, then, this was a necessary war and a just war. It is certainly true that the Allies themselves were guilty of horrible brutalities, but there is no doubt about who was on the right side in this war. Today, not only in Britain, Russia, France, Canada, China, and the United States, but also in Germany, Italy, and Japan, most people would agree that Allied victory was a necessity.

If a nation was to win in a total war it must convince its people to sacrifice. All nations used war propaganda, which simplified complex issues into simple black and white oppositions. Each asserted that it was fighting against horrendous evil. All governments censored the news; they downplayed defeats and exaggerated victories. All sought to spare their people a real sense of the brutalities of the war. In all the nations, war propaganda combined with patriotism and a sense of obligation to family, neighbors, and comrades to encourage sacrifice on the battlefield, in the factories, and at home.

There was sacrifice on all sides. It included individual heroism in foxholes, fighter planes, and submarines. For combat soldiers sacrifice meant miseries of the worst sort, far from home, bored, cold, hungry, and sometimes deathly frightened. For people on the home front the war required hard work making tanks or boots and often suffering food shortages, air raids, the death of a child, or a husband missing in action. The sacrifices of the home front and military front were connected each essential. One of the primary causes of Allied victory was that the Allied people at home mobilized to produce more and more of the stuff of war, far more by 1943 than the Axis nations.

The war ended in Europe in May 1945 and in Asia in August 1945. The Allied victors sought revenge against the defeated. One consequence was punishment of the enemy, some of whom went to the gallows or the firing squad. Great Britain and the United States also attempted eventually to rebuild the economies and to democratize the governments of Japan and Germany so that they would never again go to war. The Soviet Union's occupation of Eastern Germany

A few of the nearly 78,000 prisoners captured by the Japanese on the Bataan peninsula in April 1942 take a brief rest. Because so many of the American and Filipino prisoners died from Japanese brutality before reaching the prison camp, this tragedy became known as the Bataan Death March.

and of the whole of Eastern Europe meant a long delay in democracy in these parts of the former German Reich, and it meant the harsh decades of the Cold War. But Germany and Japan emerged as nations of peace and prosperity unimagined by the war generation. And the victorious nations created an international peacekeeping organization, the United Nations, as an effort to lessen the chances of yet another world war.

The documents in this book suggest the broad and diverse range of subjects and questions that World War II raises. The war is too large and too complex to cover all key points, but the documents that follow will encourage thinking and questioning and stimulate further learning. In these pages from history the reader will "hear" a great variety of voices from a generation that experienced firsthand the most important event of the twentieth century.

Note on Sources and Interpretation

During World War II, most people had limited information about the course of events. Military censorship closed many sources, and governments wanted to protect citizens from troubling information that might hurt morale. American newspapers and magazines in the early years of the war did not print photographs of dead U.S. soldiers. Japanese people knew so little about the war that they were shocked into silence when surrender came. In recent years the lifting of censorship has allowed libraries and archives around the world to open documents that more fully convey wartime history, including its more troubling sides.

Each period creates a different wartime history. Early students of World War II tended to focus narrowly on military and diplomatic issues. They read documents about conferences such as Yalta or leaders such as Eisenhower or Churchill. These are still essential sources. In the last few decades, however, historians have devoted great attention to social and cultural history and to sources and interpretations that go beyond men in uniform. Studying women's wartime experiences and issues of gender, for example, has produced important new insights. In the Soviet Union women became courageous pilots and expert snipers. We know more too about the important roles children played in scrap drives, ration campaigns, and other home front sacrifice. Ordinary people's letters and diaries open up new understanding. So do images in still photographs, propaganda posters, and film. Oral histories and memoirs have become particularly fruitful new sources for social and cultural subjects as well as military and diplomatic ones.

Each nation creates a different wartime history. Each tells different stories. In museums, films, and textbooks each tends to celebrate its achievements and to overlook its shortcomings. With new sources and the passage of time students can now understand global issues more clearly than twenty-five or fifty years ago. Students can see more readily the humanity on all sides, even in the midst of brutality and evil. Many war issues no longer seem so clear-cut. We can read English translations of diaries and oral histories that convey the voices and the feelings of German soldiers, Japanese mothers, and Chinese villagers.

One of the most exciting consequences of new sources and interpretations is that we can now learn more about different nations at war. Americans have a special opportunity here. The United States suffered the least in this war and emerged as the nation with the strongest military and economic power. For America this was a war of triumph. Americans have thus tended to label it a "good war" fought by the "greatest generation ever." There are arguments to support such labels. But America's good war notions sometimes grew to a myth that obscured rather than illuminated. Only recently have Americans begun to understand the meaning of forcing Japanese-American citizens into wartime concentration camps. Only gradually have many begun to question whether use of the atomic bomb against Hiroshima and Nagasaki was necessary or just. Only slowly have they begun to see that while their nation's contribution to victory was massive, and doubtless essential, others contributed as much or more. Many Americans during the long decades of the Cold War and after forgot that it was the Soviet Union that did the most difficult fighting against Nazi Germany, that more than 90 percent of the German army's total losses occurred on the Eastern Front, and that the Battle of Stalingrad might have been as important in the Axis defeat as the D-Day landings were.

Less emotional and more thoughtful analysis of sources has become easier with the passage of decades. A 1995 Smithsonian museum exhibition that told the story of the *Enola Gay* and the Hiroshima bomb revealed strong feelings and ongoing disagreements. Yet it is possible today to study sources related to Hiroshima and consider more thoughtfully the moral issues connected to killing civilians, as well as the military decisions necessary to cause Japan's surrender.

Many people who survived the war, and the Holocaust in particular, wanted to forget and to be silent. People saw the first photographs of the concentration and death camps in 1945. But not until several decades later did a growing collection of new sources force them to think about the meaning of this unfathomable tragedy. By the 1980s, oral histories, memoirs, and archival documents enabled writers, directors, and curators to tell this painful story and others in books, films, and museum exhibits.

The sources of the war years continue to demand discussion and debate. One good example is the ongoing struggle around the world to build museums, monuments, and memorials to the war generation. What kind of memorial captures the meaning of the

Holocaust or the Nanking massacre or the Japanese-American internment? In these physical forms people today continue to interpret the war, to decide what they think most important, and to commemorate what their nation or group suffered, endured, and contributed.

New sources and new interpretations have expanded, deepened, and changed what we can learn about World War II. Projects of commemoration and memory will likely continue through the century. So will the opening and creation of new sources. And so will our need to listen carefully to voices from the past and interpret them for ourselves.

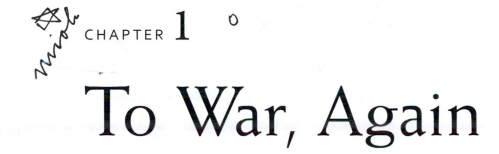

CHAPTER 1

To War, Again

Europe's two leading fascists, Italy's Benito Mussolini (left) and Germany's Adolf Hitler, parade in an open car in Munich, Germany, in June 1940. At this early point in the war, the two Axis leaders were confident of victory—a confidence reflected on their faces and in the large number of German citizens watching them go by.

Europe in the 1930s was sliding toward war. So was Asia. Instabilities and grievances covered the earth, but those with the most consequence were found in Germany, Japan, and Italy. Those three nations would become the core of the Axis powers, the aggressor nations most willing to go to war to get what they wanted. Historians continue to debate their motives and the options for resisting them.

Each aggressor nation had ambitions, deepened by the Great Depression of the 1930s. The Japanese believed that expansion into China and the rest of Asia to acquire oil, food, and raw materials was essential to their economic survival. Germany remained humiliated by the Treaty of Versailles that had ended World War I and had imposed, many Germans thought, unreasonable penalties on their defeated country. Many Germans believed that their nation needed more land and living space—Lebensraum, they called it—to grow and prosper. The Nazis were especially determined to counter the threat from the east, where the "Bolsheviks" (Soviet communists) frightened many in Europe. Italy was determined to be a world power, with colonies, military strength, and influence.

No powerful opposing nation was fully prepared prior to 1939 to stop these aggressive ambitions. The United States sat on the sidelines, with many Americans in an isolationist frame of mind, soured by memories of the Great War and protected, they thought, by vast oceans. Not until directly attacked on December 7, 1941, did the United States join the fight.

Each of the aggressor nations began in the 1930s to build military strength and to expand into neighboring countries. The Nazis

9

incorporated Austria and Czechoslovakia into their Reich; the Japanese marched into China; the Italians into Abyssinia (Ethiopia) and Albania. The process was gradual, so that no single date fully captures the start of World War II. Germany's invasion of Poland on September 1, 1939, is the best beginning date for the European war. In less than a year Germany had conquered most of Europe, culminating in the surrender of France in June 1940. Only Great Britain stood defiant. And many doubted Britain's chances. The Soviet Union, like the United States, refused to fight until it was provoked. Germans forces attacked in mid-1941.

In Asia, Japan invaded Manchuria in 1931 and then struck hard into China proper in 1937. Japanese forces moved south into French Indochina in 1940 and prepared to expand across Southeast Asia and the Pacific. The attack on Pearl Harbor on December 7, 1941, was a crucial part of that expansion, marked also by the defeat of the British in Singapore and of the Americans in the Philippines.

These were glorious days for the Axis nations, as they acquired territory they thought so essential to their economic and national greatness. They were very dark days for those nations that would eventually unite as the Allied powers in order to beat back the aggressors.

Great War

The 1914–1918 war was usually called the Great War until another great war began in 1939, which led to the renaming of this war as World War I.

These British Spitfire fighter planes and their pilots shot down and drove back many German bombers over England, a major reason Hitler's plan to invade Britain failed. As the air battle raged in summer 1940, Churchill said of these airmen that "never in the field of human conflict was so much owed by so many to so few."

Aggressor Nations

Germany, Italy, and Japan were united by a disdain for democracy, professing instead the special and superior qualities of their people, often in racial terms, and an unquestioning dedication to the will of their respective leaders. No twentieth-century figure had more enthusiastic followers than Adolf Hitler, head of the Nazi Party, who from 1933 to his death in 1945 was simply "Der Fuhrer" (the leader). William Shirer, an astute American journalist stationed in Berlin, assessed Hitler's power in a diary entry of December 1, 1940. Shirer likely exaggerated this one man's power, since so many other Germans contributed to the triumphs and tragedies of the Third Reich. Scholars continue to debate the nature of popular support for Hitler, but none doubt it was real and substantial in 1940.

I suppose the reasons why Germany has embarked on a career of unbridled conquest do go deeper than the mere fact, all-important though it is, that a small band of unprincipled, tough gangsters have seized control of this land, corrupted its whole people, and driven it on its present course. The roots go deeper, I admit, though whether the plant would have flowered as it has without Hitler, I seriously doubt. . . .

It is the evil genius of Adolf Hitler that has aroused this basic feeling and given it tangible expression. It is due to this remarkable and terrifying man alone that the German dream now stands such a fair chance of coming true. First Germans and then the world grossly underestimated him. It was an appalling error, as first Germans and now the world are finding out. Today, so far as the vast majority of his fellow countrymen are concerned, he has reached a pinnacle never before achieved by a German ruler. He has become—even before his death—a myth, a legend, almost a god, with that quality of divinity which the Japanese people ascribe to their Emperor. To many Germans he is a figure remote, unreal, hardly human. For them he has become infallible. They say, as many peoples down through history have said of their respective gods: "He is always right."

Notwithstanding many reports to the contrary which float abroad, he is the sole and absolute boss of Germany today, brooking no interference from anyone and rarely asking and almost never heeding suggestions from his intimidated lieutenants. The men around him are all loyal, all afraid, and none of them are his friends. He has no friends. . . .

Hitler and the National Socialist Party, or Nazis, wanted to build an empire that would last a thousand years. In the *Frauen-Warte* (*Women's Viewpoint*), a Nazi magazine for German women, an unidentified writer in 1937 made clear the special nature of the German people and pointed to key themes in Nazi ideology, including the need to educate youth to fight and die for their nation. It was a high ideal, the writer claimed, that only "pure" Germans could understand.

National Socialist education is an education in the thinking of the German people, in understanding German traditions, in awakening the pure, uncorrupted and honest people's consciousness, their sense of belonging to the people. Only a pure member of the German race can have such an understanding of his people, crowning it with the willingness to sacrifice all for the people. He must know that without

Japan's Prediction for Democracy

In the battle between democracy and totalitarianism the latter adversary will without question win and will control the world. The era of democracy is finished and the democratic system bankrupt. There is not room in the world for two different systems or for two different economies. . . . Fascism will develop in Japan through the people's will. It will come out of love for the Emperor.

—Japanese Foreign Minister Matsuoka Yosuke, in an interview with the *New York Herald Tribune* on July 21, 1940

Fascism's promise of strong leadership appealed to Nogi Harumichi, a Japanese student when the war began. Years later in an oral history interview he recalled that "I bought Hitler's heroic autobiography *Mein Kampf*. Japanese youth at that time adored Hitler and Mussolini and yearned for the emergence of a Japanese politician with the same qualities. We wanted decisive action."

African-American runner Jesse Owens (center) salutes the American flag after receiving the first of his four gold medals, in the long jump, at the 1936 Olympic Games. The silver medal went to the German Lutz Long (right), who gives the Nazi salute. Because these Olympics were held in Berlin, Owens's celebrated victories became a slap in the face to Nazi notions of racial superiority.

his people he is a miserable nothing, and that it is better if he himself die than that his people and fatherland perish!

He who thinks that National Socialist education has as its goal a kind of hyper-patriotism has not understood it. Something entirely different is intended. Something should be awakened in the soul of young Germans that will fill their hearts and whole being until their souls can no longer restrain the overflowing, until a powerful and jubilant "Hail Germany" springs from their lips! That call itself is not the first or most significant goal: rather it is its foundation in the soul, a foundation that jubilantly, freely, confidently, cheerfully and passionately expresses itself. It is the holy sense of people and fatherland!

Awakening this in the German youth requires that they have a clear understanding of the value of people and fatherland. They must realize that the German people has a right to independence and freedom, honor and power. They must learn that it has a right to its own fate among the peoples of the earth, and it must gain with the other peoples the place in the sun that belongs to it. It must do this not through force, rather because the German people is a noble nation that has created values for the entire world that no other people was capable of. We want to awaken in the German youth this free, righteous and noble national pride so that at the thought of Germany's past, present and future their hearts will pound and their eyes will gleam. That is the first foundation of National Socialist education.

It is clear that the German youth must be resolved to defend their fatherland with their lives. Despite all the nonsense about promises and disarmament, Germany is surrounded by weapons. The German youth must learn military virtues. Their bodies must be steeled, made hard and strong, so that the youth may become capable soldiers who are healthy, strong, trained, energetic and able to bear hardships. Gymnastics, games, sports, hiking, swimming, and military exercises must all be learned by the youth. Our youth should not sit in stuffy rooms and develop crooked backs and weak eyes. Alongside the basic and truly important education of the mind, they should develop healthy bodies by being outdoors.

The idea of the healthy and strong German should not be mere empty talk. Parents can help here. They will train our youth in simplicity and cleanliness. They will train them, even when they are older, not to waste their spare time by dubious or even harmful activities such as card playing, drinking alcohol and bad music, rather to prepare their bodies for their future tasks.

Those people whom the Nazis judged as not of "pure" German blood were deemed lesser peoples. At the bottom of the Nazi hierarchy were Jews. At a Nazi rally in the city of Nuremberg, the government announced its "Law for the Protection of German Blood and German Honor," dated September 15, 1935. The law excluded Jews from citizenship, prohibited "racial mixing," and took early steps that would end in policies of extermination.

The headline of this 1938 poster promotes, as "The Book of the Germans," Hitler's autobiography, *Mein Kampf*. The text at the bottom claims sales of four million copies.

Convinced of the truth that the purity of German blood is the necessary condition for the continued existence of the German people, and animated by the inflexible determination to safeguard the German nation for all time, the Reichstag has unanimously decreed the following law, which is hereby announced:

#1 (1) Marriages between Jews and citizens of German or kindred blood are forbidden. Marriages concluded in defiance of this law are void, even if, for the purpose of evading this law, they are concluded abroad.

 (2) Proceedings for annulment may be initiated only by the Public Prosecutor.

#2 Extra-marital intercourse between Jews and citizens of German or kindred blood is forbidden.

#3 Jews may not employ female citizens of German or kindred blood under the age of 45 in their households.

#4 (1) Jews are forbidden to hoist the Reich and national flag and to display the colors of the Reich.

 (2) On the other hand, the display of the Jewish colors is permitted. The practice of this authorization is protected by the State.

#5 (1) Whoever acts contrary to the prohibition of #1 will be punished by penitentiary.

 (2) The man who acts contrary to the prohibition of # 2 will be punished by jail or penitentiary.

 (3) Whoever acts contrary to the provisions of #3 or #4 will be punished by imprisonment up to one year and with a fine or with one of these penalties.

Hitler's prejudice extended beyond Jews to include the United States. One of his close associates was Albert Speer, who served as minister of armaments and munitions. At the end of the war Speer was an Allied prisoner at a British-controlled prison in central Germany given the code name of "Dustbin" (the counterpart American prison was code-named "Ashcan"). In this transcript of an interrogation made there on September 7, 1945, Speer describes Hitler and his fellow Nazis as narrow-minded men with a very limited view of the world from their grand headquarters (called the Reichskanzlei).

Q: What was the part of the United States in pre-war German plans and speculations?

Speer: There were no men capable of world-wide thinking in Reichskanzlei. The group which gathered there had never got beyond Germany. It counted for something if one of them had been on a vacation trip to Italy. Hitler himself had seen nothing of the world and had no first-hand knowledge of foreign countries. He thought of England in terms of an island state. He underestimated the power of the [British] Empire, and much more of the USA.

There were two men who attempted to influence Hitler, one of them being his second Adjutant, [Fritz] Wiedemann, who would insist on starting political discussions about America, urging that it should be possible to establish connections there. Hitler got so annoyed with him that he sent him as Consul-General to San Francisco—a kind of punitive transfer—and told him that he should cure himself of his ideas. Hitler was convinced that there was no possibility of collaboration with America. Incidentally, he would never believe that there was a unified American nation, a new people such as we have come to know it now. He regarded America as a mass of individual immigrants as yet not fully consolidated.

Q: Didn't he draw any conclusions from America's entry into the First World War?

Speer: He did not think much of that. He said that the Americans had not been particularly prominent then, and had made no great sacrifices in blood. They were not a tough nation, and if put to the test, they would be found not to be a closely-knit nation in the European sense. He retained this view during the war, when assessing the military valor of the Americans. He predicted that they would turn out to be poor fighters who could not stand up to a serious test. This, of course, was the

I'm not interested in politics. The problems of the world are not in my department.

—Rick (played by Humphrey Bogart), in the 1942 film *Casablanca*, expressing the isolationist feelings of many Americans before Pearl Harbor basic idea behind the Ardennes offensive [the Battle of the Bulge, December 1944], and the hopes which Hitler placed upon it. He also expected that any great sacrifices demanded from the Americans would result in serious domestic political complications.

On November 18, 1937, as Japan's troops marched into China, Richard Storry, a young Englishman teaching school in northern Japan and an admirer of the Japanese people, wrote sadly to his parents. Unlike many of his students, Storry saw that the glory of conquest would have a tragic ending.

This war is totally worked up by the military clique, who have the main power in this country. There can be no moral justification for the invasion of China. . . . At the beginning, in July [1937], one heard criticisms of the aggressive policy against China, some students here wrote an article in the college paper attacking the government of its "fascism." This caused a stir, and since then students, whom I know well, have said how much they disliked the power of the military, but it is not safe to rely on these signs of dissatisfaction. The country at large, with the successful war on, supports the government. . . . Intelligent Japanese, who in their hearts condemn the war, cannot protest. The Conservatives like it because it rouses the "National Spirit" and develops Emperor worship. The army likes it because they like fighting. Big business imagines it will get rich by the war and young men have no idea, as a whole, of criticizing their elders whom from youth up they are taught to regard as their betters. The women of course don't count. . . .

As I look at my students, either in a lecture room or as they drill and do manoeuvres in the snow, my heart aches at the pity of this war, and the wars that will come upon them. But they think it no tragedy, their greatest glory is to die in the service of the Emperor, collectively they become a very terrible fighting machine, and as they die they shout "Banzai, long live the Emperor."

The panic and flight of enemy invasion has begun as Chinese civilians, many with a few hastily gathered belongings, clog this Shanghai street in 1937. Soon after the city would fall to the Japanese invaders.

Japanese troops conquered the Chinese city of Nanking in late 1937. They brutalized and murdered large numbers of captured Chinese soldiers and civilians. An American doctor at the city's University Hospital, Robert Wilson, wrote his family on December 18, 1937, providing details of the horror he witnessed. The Nanking Massacre remains a major source of tension between China and Japan.

Today marks the sixth day of the modern Dante's Inferno, written in huge letters with blood and rape. Murder by the wholesale and rape by the thousands of cases. There seems to be no stop to the ferocity, lust and atavism of the brutes. At first I tried to be pleasant to them to avoid arousing their ire but the smile has gradually worn off and my stare is fully as cool and fishy as theirs....

Let me recount some instances occurring in the last two days. Last night the house of one of the Chinese staff member of the university was broken into and two of the women, his relatives, were raped. Two girls about 16 were raped to death in one of the refugee camps. In the University Middle School where there are 8,000 people the Japs came in ten times last night, over the wall, stole food, clothing, and raped until they were satisfied. They bayoneted one little boy, killing him, and I spent an hour an a half this morning patching up another little boy of eight who had five bayonet wounds....

Nanking's Massacre Memorial Hall shows at its entrance the Chinese claim for the number killed by the Japanese—300,000 victims. Tensions over the Nanking Massacre of 1937 soured relations between China and Japan into the twenty-first century. Some in Japan denied that a massacre occurred; some claimed that Japanese troops killed only a few thousand Chinese.

From Appeasement to War

German, Italian, and Japanese conquest in the 1930s deeply troubled other nations. Some, such as China, were militarily weak and could slow but not stop Japanese aggression. The western democracies had more military power but hoped that Germany's claims for territory could be appeased. At a meeting in Munich, Germany, in 1938, British Prime Minister Neville Chamberlain thought he had convinced Hitler to end his territorial expansion by permitting him to occupy parts of Czechoslovakia. There would be "peace for our time," Chamberlain said. The Soviet Union also wanted to avoid war with Germany, but shared with the Nazis a desire for more territory. In the Nazi-Soviet Pact of 1939 the two nations agreed they would not attack each other—and would divide up Poland and expand elsewhere. This cynical arrangement shocked the world. Writing from London, a reporter for the *New York Times* conveyed the anger and fear of a "Reich Dominant in Europe."

LONDON, Aug. 21.—The deadliest high explosives could not have caused more damage in London than the news late tonight that the Nazi and Soviet Governments had agreed on a non-aggression pact behind the backs of the British and French military missions in Moscow.

Anger and stupefaction were the first reactions here. They were all the more intense because neither of the Western governments appeared to have had any inkling of what was impending. It will take some time for the smoke to clear away, but when it does the diplomatic picture may well be changed beyond all recognition.

First impressions were that the Russian-German pact would complete the encirclement of Poland by showing that Russian help would not be forthcoming in the event of invasion and that it would make continuance of the three-power talks in Moscow difficult if not impossible. Moreover, the news conjured up the specter, always dreaded in this country, of Germany and Russia, as allies, dividing the Baltic States and Eastern Europe between them.

Nazi Triumph of the First Rank

Such speculation may prove to be too highly colored, but there could be no doubt tonight that Britain had suffered a humiliation of the first order and that German diplomacy had won one of its biggest triumphs. It remains to be seen how the anti-aggression "front" will survive this bombshell, especially in view of Russia's close relations with Turkey and her long frontier with Rumania.

Prime Minister Chamberlain and his Ministerial colleagues will feel the full shock of the news from Berlin when they meet tomorrow afternoon in a full-fledged Cabinet meeting originally intended to cope with the danger of a German invasion of Poland. All day today there had been signs of a swiftly developing crisis, with ominous reports from Berlin, Prague, Vienna, Bratislava and other cities of vast numbers of German troops on the move eastward.

It had been intended that after the Cabinet meeting Viscount Halifax, the Foreign Secretary, might make a statement over the radio repeating once more and in most detailed terms that Britain would fight in fulfillment of her pledges whenever the Poles felt that their independence was threatened. The general idea was not only to repeat the explicit terms of the British guarantee but also to recall Mr. Chamberlain's warning of last year that Britain would fight any attempt to "dominate Europe by force."

Germany's invasion of Poland on September 1, 1939, meant war. Britain and France had earlier promised support for Polish independence. On

We were devoted to this country, Poland. We were very great patriots. And we felt secure. We thought that if something happened, if war would break out, England and France and the U.S. would come to our help. We thought we would be the winners, not the losers. We never for one second believed that we would lose the war, that the Germans would take over Poland. But within a few days, the Polish soldiers were already dirty, raggedy, disorganized. They looked already like they had been fighting for years. When I looked at them, I said, we're going to win this war? Then I knew, we're not going to win any war.

—Felicia Fuksman, remembering in an oral history interview in 1989 her feelings as a Polish teenager in September 1939

September 3, 1939, Prime Minister Chamberlain made a cheerless radio address to the British people.

I am speaking to you from the Cabinet Room at 10, Downing Street.

This morning the British Ambassador in Berlin handed the German Government a final Note stating that unless we heard from them by 11 o'clock that they were prepared at once to withdraw their troops from Poland a state of war would exist between us. I have to tell you now that no such undertaking has been received, and that consequently this country is at war with Germany.

You can imagine what a bitter blow it is to me that all my long struggle to win peace has failed. Yet I cannot believe that there is anything more or anything different that I could have done and that would have been more successful.

Up to the very last it would have been quite possible to have arranged a peaceful and honourable settlement between Germany and Poland. But Hitler would not have it. He had evidently made up his mind to attack Poland whatever happened, and although he now says he put forward reasonable proposals which were rejected by the Poles, that is not a true statement. The proposals were never shown to the Poles, nor to us, and, though they were announced in a German broadcast on Thursday night, Hitler did not wait to hear comments on them, but ordered his troops to cross the Polish frontier. His action shows convincingly that there is no chance of expecting that this man will ever give up his practice of using force to gain his will. He can only be stopped by force.

We and France are to-day, in fulfillment of our obligations, going to the aid of Poland, who is so bravely resisting this wicked and unprovoked attack upon her people. We have a clear conscience. We have done all that any country could do to establish peace, but a situation in which no word given by Germany's ruler could be trusted and no people or country could feel themselves safe had become intolerable. And now that we have resolved to finish it, I know that you will all play your part with calmness and courage.

As such a moment as this the assurances of support that we have received from the Empire are a source of profound encouragement to us.

. . . Now may God bless you all and may He defend the right. For it is evil things that we shall be fighting against, brute force, bad faith, injustice, oppression and persecution. And against them I am certain that the right will prevail.

A few months after Chamberlain's address, the world would see a fore-telling of the terror the Nazis would spread across the continent. The *Times* of London reported on March 1, 1940, what the Germans had done to Polish universities as part of their determination to destroy a Slavic culture they deemed inferior.

The methods applied by the Germans in Poland against the universities and their academicians prove that Germany aims at a complete annihilation of Polish intellectual life and scientific institutions. In their violence these methods have hardly been surpassed in modern civilization. . . . Everything is being destroyed which might contribute to the culture of the Polish people. The Universities of Cracow, Warsaw, Lublin, and Poznan are enveloped in this ruin.

The University of Cracow, established in 1364, is one of the oldest in the world. Coupled with the Cracow Academy of Science and Letters, the university was the most important centre of Polish intellectual life. This was apparently reason enough why it should be singled out by the Nazis in their destructive activity. . . . On the pretext that their presence was required at a conference, 170 professors were summoned to the University Hall. The chief of the Gestapo, one Meyer, addressed the professors in the German language. He declared that since they had tried to reopen the university without authority, had continued their work in its scientific institutions, and were arranging for examinations of the undergraduates without German permission all professors present in the hall were arrested.

Moved by the German bombing of the Spanish town of Guernica, one of the twentieth century's greatest artists portrayed the suffering of war in the painting *Guernica* (1937). Pablo Picasso depicted the shrieking woman, the horse, and the bull in an abstract style that conveys the pain of war more forcefully than the sharpest photograph could. There was worse to come in the way of aerial bombing and civilian pain, yet this painting remains its most powerful image.

The professors were deported to <u>concentration camps</u> in Germany, most of them to the camp of Sachsenhausen, near Oranienburg. . . . Nine of the professors imprisoned at Sachsenhausen have died, but there is every reason to fear that the death-roll will not end with these nine victims of oppression.

Japan's ambition matched Germany's, but Westerners were slow to see Japan's military strength. One respected American writer, Fletcher Pratt, analyzed Japanese military capability in a book titled *Sea Power and History*, published in 1939. Many Americans shared Pratt's ignorance about Japan and also his cultural and racial provincialism. The nation was unprepared for an attack from Japan.

They can neither make good airplanes nor fly them well, in spite of the most heroic efforts. . . .

Every observer concurs in the opinion that the Japanese are daring but incompetent aviators; hardly any two agree on the reason. Four main theories have been advanced, explaining it on (a) medical, (b) religious, (c) psychological and (d) educational grounds.

According to the first postulate the <u>Japanese as a race</u> have defects of the tubes of the inner ear, just as they are generally myopic. This gives them a defective sense of balance, the one physical sense in which an aviator is not permitted to be deficient.

The second explanation places the blame on Bushido and the Japanese code that the individual life is valueless. Therefore, when the plane gets into a spin or some other trouble, they are apt to fold their hands across their stomachs and die cheerfully for the glory of the Empire. . . .

The psychological theory points out that the Japanese, even more than the Germans, are people of combination. "Nothing is much stupider than one Japanese, and nothing much brighter than two." But the aviator is peculiarly alone, and the Japanese, poor individualists, are thus poor aviators.

Finally the educational explanation points out that Japanese children receive fewer mechanical toys and less mechanical training than those of any other race.

On a Japanese aircraft carrier the cheers of the crew and the flag of the rising sun send planes toward Pearl Harbor on December 7, 1941.

Bushido
Bushido is the traditional Japanese way of the warrior, which glorifies death in war.

Whichever be true, the Japanese remain poor aviators. . . .

Japan dares provoke or enter no war in which the United States fleet will be engaged on the opposite side.

These "poor aviators" of Imperial Japan took off from their carriers to carry out one of the most daring and successful military attacks in world history. As Americans heard the news from Pearl Harbor that Sunday, December 7, 1941, they were shocked and bewildered and then angry. That evening Rubye Seago, a young woman in Lawrence-ville, Virginia, wrote her boyfriend, Richard Long, who was then in basic training in Georgia.

Lawrenceville, Sunday Nite,
Dec. 7, 1941

My Darling,

I know you feel exactly like I do right now. I've just been listening to the radio. I've never been so blue or heartsick as I am right this minute. Oh, my darling—if it were possible I'd charter a plane—do anything—just to see you for a few minutes. . . .

Honestly, Dick, if I don't get to see you I'm going to lose my mind. Isn't there *any* thing you can do? 'Cause if you don't do it now do you realize we may *never* see each other again? Of course you do—you realize how serious the situation is, even more than I.

Darling, they *can't* take you—the finest, sweetest boy that ever lived and send you away—it just tears my heart out to think of it.

Everyone in town is talking war, war, war! Everyone is sure it will be declared tomorrow. There are some sad hearts over this world tonight. And none sadder than mine. And your poor mother. . . .

Please don't let anything happen without letting me know. Wire me or call me or something. If it's possible.

Forever yours, Rubye

What a day—the incredulousness of it all still gives each new announcement the unreality of a fairy tale. How can they have been so mad?

Navy pilot Bill Evans, Jr., in a letter to his parents, December 7, 1941

The *USS Shaw* explodes during the Japanese attack on Pearl Harbor. The *Shaw* was one of three destroyers, along with five battleships, sunk that Sunday morning in a surprise attack that this generation of Americans would never forget.

Rubye Seago accurately predicted the beginning of war for America. The next day, December 8, President Franklin D. Roosevelt went to the Capitol to ask Congress to declare war. The first page of the working draft of his speech to Congress shows revisions the president made, including changing the words "world history" to "infamy." Millions of Americans heard the speech on radio. Few ever forgot Pearl Harbor.

President Franklin D. Roosevelt signs the Declaration of War against Japan on December 8, 1941. Congress had approved his request for the declaration immediately; the Pearl Harbor attack had eliminated American debate over going to war.

Joseph Goebbels, the German propaganda minister, was elated with the news of Pearl Harbor. In his diary on December 8, 1941, he wrote:

The Japanese followed a very resolute tactic in unleashing this conflict. They simply pounced on the enemy that wanted to strangle them and attacked him. I trust that the Japanese still have a few things in reserve; for they generally pursue very cautious, traditionally conservative policies; they will not negligently risk their empire, and they surely have a whole series of military options, about which even we know nothing. They did not inform us in advance of their intention to attack suddenly, and this was also necessary to maintain the secrecy of their plans.

All these events are still rather unclear for the time being. But the war is a fact. [Prime Minister] Tojo was more dependable after all than we had assumed at first. The Fuhrer and the whole headquarters are overjoyed at this development. We are now at least temporarily secure from a serious threat. In the coming weeks and months Roosevelt will no longer be as insolent as he has been in the past.

Now this war has become a world war in the true sense of the word. Beginning for the slightest of reasons, it is now creating ramifications all over the globe. More even than before it offers us a great national opportunity. Now it all depends on our seeing the thing through and maintaining composure in every crisis that may come. If we win this conflict, then there is no more impediment to the realization of the German dream of world power. We want to venture everything to achieve this goal. The opportunities have never been as favorable as today. It is essential to take advantage of them.

And on December 10, 1941, after meeting with Hitler, Goebbels recorded in his diary the gist of Hitler's words.

At the start of the war, the Japanese Zero was one of the finest fighter planes in the world. Its agility and firepower and its well-trained pilots earned respect and fear. As American pilots and planes improved, however, the Zero's days, like those of the Japanese Empire, were numbered.

The Fuhrer maintains that the Japanese fleet in the Pacific is far superior to the Anglo-American fleet, especially after its early successes against the US fleet. The Japanese made a great start and can now dominate the Pacific Ocean almost without limit. There is scarcely a challenger in sight here any longer. The Japanese adopted an absolutely correct tactic by immediately mounting an attack and not getting involved in long preliminaries preceding the outbreak of war. Undoubtedly now the Japanese will take up the fight for the US bases in the Pacific first, and they will do this, judging by their whole character, very systematically, taking one base after another either by destroying or capturing it. Both the Americans and the English are thereby faced with the cruel fact that their influence in the Pacific will be lost altogether.

Dark Days for the Allies

With their speed, superior equipment, and advantage of surprise, the Axis aggressors moved from victory to victory. A quick, short war was their hope and goal. In Europe, the Germans moved west after conquering Poland. France fell in June 1940. Looking through a dusty window, American journalist William Shirer observed the French surrender ceremony held in a very special railway car. Shirer recorded what he saw in this diary entry of June 21, 1940.

Plenipotentiaries
Plenipotentiaries are official representatives of their governments.

On the exact spot in the little clearing in the Forest of Compiègne where at five A.M. on November 11, 1918 the armistice which ended the World War was signed, Adolf Hitler today handed *his* armistice terms to France. To make German revenge complete, the meeting of the German and French plenipotentiaries took place in Marshal [Ferdinand] Foch's private car, in which Foch [Allied military commander] laid down the armistice terms to Germany twenty-two years ago. Even the same table in the rickety old *wagon-lit* car was used. And through the windows we saw Hitler occupying the very seat on which Foch had sat at that table when he dictated the other armistice.

The humiliation of France, of the French, was complete. And yet in the preamble to the armistice terms Hitler told the French that he had not chosen this spot at Compiègne out of revenge: merely to right an old wrong. From the demeanour of the French delegates I gathered that they did not appreciate the difference . . .

At three forty-two P.M., twelve minutes after the French arrive, we see Hitler stand up, salute stiffly, and then stride out of the drawing-room. . . .

Hitler and his aides stride down the avenue . . . where their cars are waiting. As they pass the guard of honour, the German band strikes up the two national anthems, *Deutschland, Deutschland über Alles* and the *Horst Wessel* song. The whole ceremony in which Hitler has reached a new pinnacle in his meteoric career and Germany avenged the 1918 defeat is over in a quarter of an hour.

With France defeated and Paris occupied by German troops, Great Britain stood alone in Europe. Hitler prepared to invade the island nation, beginning with aerial bombardment. Alan Brooke was the British military officer responsible for home defense. His diary entries in September 1940 reveal the fears he could not show others.

NICKY

French citizens watch victorious German soldiers march into Paris on June 14, 1940. Few expected France to fall so quickly. The tears of that day, shown on the face of one citizen, would last a long time.

8 September

Heavy bombing of London throughout the night, the whole sky being lit up by the glow of fires in London docks. Went to the office in the morning where I found further indications of impending invasion. . . .

15 September

Still no move on the part of the Germans! Everything remains keyed up for an early invasion, and the air war goes on unabated. The coming week must remain a critical one, and it is hard to see how Hitler can now retrace his steps and stop the invasions. The suspense of waiting is very trying especially when one is familiar with the weakness of our defence! . . .

A responsibility such as that of defence of this country under the existing conditions is one that weighs on one like a ton of bricks, and it is hard at times to retain the hopeful, confident exterior which is so essential to retain the confidence of those under one, and to guard against their having any doubts as regards final success.

Fortunately, for Brooke and all of Britain, the Germans gave up their planned invasion and in June 1941 turned on the Soviet Union. Meanwhile,

We shall not flag or fail. We shall go on to the end. We shall fight in France, we shall fight on the seas and oceans, we shall fight with growing confidence and growing strength in the air, we shall defend our island, whatever the cost may be. We shall fight on the beaches, we shall fight on the landing grounds, we shall fight in the fields and in the streets, we shall fight in the hills; we shall never surrender.

—British Prime Minister Winston Churchill, speech to the House of Commons, June 4, 1940 the Japanese were moving toward control of large portions of Asia and the Pacific. Prime Minister Hideki Tojo addressed Japan's legislature, The Diet, on May 27, 1942, boasting of military success. The translator of Tojo's words left readers a stilted version, but his arrogance comes through.

By the close and joint operation of Imperial army and naval forces the southwestern Pacific has completely fallen into our control. Australia has become the orphan of the Pacific Ocean. Especially only recently in the Coral Sea battle carried out on the northern tip of Australia the American and British sea power has been crushed, and now there is no one before us to defend Australia. At this time I should like to emphasize again anew what I have said once before in the previous Diet meeting to the leaders of Australia that they should survey the international situation, take into consideration Australia's geographical [jurisdiction], and decide upon their measures of disposal which at the present time is most important. At the present time, India is in confusion and in an unsettled state, Chungking is about to collapse, and Australia is isolated. As I review Shonan, Hongkong, and other important bases, peace and order being restored are steadily becoming the (foundation) of Greater East Asia establishment and are making great strides in its rebirth. Our sea power in the Pacific and the Indian Ocean is expanding day

A company of poorly equipped Chinese soldiers attempts to stop a charge of 50,000 Japanese in Burma in 1943. Chinese, British, Indian, West African, and other soldiers joined against the Japanese invaders in one of the longest land campaigns of the war. Not until August 1945 did Japan surrender in Burma.

by day. Contrary to this, Britain has lost [its] overseas possessions and the route by which natural resources have been obtained has been taken control of by our forces. As a result it has added a great strain on British domestic politics, and at the present time, Britain has reached a point of collapse. On the other hand, America that is suffering repeated defeats is trying to cover its mortal blow by relying on vicious propaganda and is in a desperate condition trying to cover the rising criticism within the country and to preserve the right of neutral countries. . . .

Imperial Japan has firm confidence in the attainment of the ultimate victory in this sacred war, and our military operations which are magnificent and unparalleled in this world are being boldly expanded. Hereafter, the Government has high hopes in the fulfillment of the Imperial wishes by attaining complete unity with the people, by managing the improvement and expansion of the total war effort of the nation, and by so doing tightening the strings of the helmet so that we may display ever more the ideal fighting spirit which is inherent of Imperial Japan and we may quickly bring about the fulfillment of our mission in the Holy War.

CHAPTER **2**

Fighting Men and Women

The shrouded bodies of officers and sailors killed by a Japanese bomb on the USS *Intrepid* receive a burial at sea off the Philippines in November 1944. This ancient and somber service usually begins with the command "All hands bury the dead" and ends with the firing of three volleys and the playing of taps.

In countries all over the world men went off to war. Combat was an experience none would forget. Often war was boring: long days standing in lines, no news from home, and nothing to do. Sometimes war was mostly about keeping feet dry or finding enough to eat or a place to sleep out of the rain or cold. And sometimes war was a terror unimagined even by those who had so eagerly marched off to fight. Too often, it was everything contained in the phrase "war is hell."

The nature of the fighting differed, but as the war proceeded it became more harsh and terrible. There were rules of war, written and unwritten. Some applied to proper treatment for prisoners of war, for example, including requirements that they have decent food, medical care, and housing. In the fighting on the Western Front the British, Americans, Canadians, Italians, and Germans generally followed these agreed-upon rules. Elsewhere, war moved to escalating brutality, to a war without limits and without mercy. On the Eastern Front the Soviet Red Army and the Germans often engaged in brutalities that included murdering prisoners of war. So too in Asia and the Pacific.

In many cultures combat was a role many people deemed inappropriate for women. Men were obligated to protect women, who were to focus on home and family responsibilities. The necessities of war pushed against such traditional gender roles, however, so in many nations women entered military service and even, in some, engaged in combat.

Men and Women in War

World War II produced thousands of acts of courage and bravery on all sides. One war hero was a young naval lieutenant from Massachusetts named John F. Kennedy. Commanding a Motor Torpedo Boat (PT 109) sunk by the Japanese, Kennedy suffered an injury that plagued him all the way to the presidency. In a military hospital in June 1944 Kennedy received the Navy and Marine Corps Medal, a Purple Heart, and this citation.

For heroism in the rescue of 3 men following the ramming and sinking of his motor torpedo boat while attempting a torpedo attack on a Japanese destroyer in the Solomon Islands area on the night of Aug 1–2, 1943. Lt. KENNEDY, Capt. of the boat, directed the rescue of the crew and personally rescued 3 men, one of whom was seriously injured. During the following 6 days, he succeeded in getting his crew ashore, and after swimming many hours attempting to secure aid and food, finally effected the rescue of the men. His courage, endurance and excellent leadership contributed to the saving of several lives and was in keeping with the highest traditions of the United States Naval Service.

Lt. John F. Kennedy (far right) and his crew on board PT109 in 1943. Later, when he entered politics, Kennedy was asked how he became a hero. His laconic response: "It was involuntary. They sank my boat."

America went to war with a segregated military—a separation of blacks from whites that reflected the segregation at home. Denied combat assignments at first, African Americans drove trucks, cooked food on ships, and performed other menial chores, as they generally did at home. Protest against this injustice led to the formation of an all-black unit of fighter pilots known as the Tuskegee Airmen. Could blacks perform in combat?

Charles McGee, flying in *Kitten*, a plane he named for his wife, was one of many who proved that black pilots could fight. In an interview published in 1999 he recalled—with the aid of his flight log—a mission over Czechoslovakia in 1944.

We were pretty much over the target area when we spotted a Focke Wulf Fw-190 and I got the word, "Go get him." I fell in behind him, and he took all kinds of evasive action, diving for the ground. We were down over the local airfield—I remember seeing a hangar on fire out of the corner of my eye—when I got in behind him and got in a burst that must have hit something in the controls. He took a couple more hard evasive turns and then went right into the ground. I stayed low getting out, to stay out of the sights of enemy ground-fire. During that time, I saw a train pulling into a little station, so I dropped my nose and made a firing pass at the engine. Then, when I thought I'd pulled away from where I thought all the ack-ack was, I began climbing back up. [Roger] Romine was my wingman on that occasion, and somewhere in all that jinking he had lost me and had gone up to rejoin the formation. He saw the Fw-190 crash, though, and confirmed the victory for me. . . .

I flew a total of 136 [missions], of which 82 were tactical and 54 were long-range, high-altitude missions. I flew my last mission over Brux, Germany, on November 17, 1944, and it was a long one—about five hours, 45 minutes. Then, on November 23, I was shipped back to Tuskegee to replace a white twin-engine instructor. . . . My *Kitten* went to the 301st Squadron, was renumbered 51 and flown by Lieutenant Leon Speers, who was shot down on April 24, 1945, and taken prisoner.

Many nations allowed women to serve in the military, but often only in supportive roles. In 1941 Britain began drafting women. A British Information Service pamphlet of November 1943 described the Auxiliary Territorial Service (ATS), the army unit for women, and explained where the gender line was drawn.

The Auxiliary Territorial Service, the Women's Auxiliary Air Force and the Women's Royal Naval Service are organizations that recruit women to replace men for non-combatant duties with the Army, Air Force, and Navy respectively. In all three Services uniform and full equipment is furnished and the rate of pay is about two-thirds that of a man, according to rank. All educational facilities available to men in the Forces are also open to women. Members of all three Services undertake duties at home and overseas. . . .

At the outbreak of the war women in the A.T.S. were employed in only 4 trades, but the number has now risen to 63. They work, for example, as switchboard and teleprinter operators, kine-theodolite operators [measuring hits on targets], dispatch riders, cooks, draughtsmen, orderlies; they may work on experimental ranges, in gunnery research, on anti-aircraft duties, and on radiolocation duties, and with searchlight batteries.

ATS women spotters use identification telescopes at an anti-aircraft gun site in London in September 1941. Using women so close to danger was controversial but eventually deemed essential in the hard fight against Germany.

Soldiers Bathing,
by F. T. Prince (1942)

The sea at evening moves across the sand.
Under a reddening sky I watch the
    freedom of a band
Of soldiers who belong to me. Stripped
    bare
For bathing in the sea, they shout and
    run in the warm air;
Their flesh worn by the trade of war,
    revives
And my mind towards the meaning of
    it strives.

Thousands of women are serving guns alongside men, working predictors under fire in anti-aircraft batteries. Members of the A.T.S. take over almost every duty with these batteries except the actual operating and firing of the gun itself; their primary function is to work the instruments by which the target is located and order the firing.

In some nations women entered combat. The most decorated women's unit in the Soviet Union was the 46th Guards Bomber Regiment, known to the Germans as the "night witches." They flew 24,000 combat missions, mostly at night in flimsy airplanes. Thirty of them perished; twenty-three were decorated as Heroes of the Soviet Union. One of the decorated Heroes was Polina Gelman, who described her work to an interviewer in 1990.

We hated the German fascists so much that we didn't care which aircraft we were to fly: we would have even flown a broom to be able to fire at them! But we didn't fly brooms: we were given a biplane, the PO-2, to do our night bombing, without even any optical sights to indicate when to drop the bombs. Instead, we devised a method of visual sighting by making a chalk mark on the wing of the aircraft to indicate when to drop the bombs. This sight was unique in that each of us, being of different heights, would make a mark in a slightly different place—a personalized mark, it could be called—to help us in bombing accurately. . . .

The slow speed of this aircraft, only 100 kilometers per hour, made us a target from both small-arms fire and antiaircraft guns. The plane was covered with fabric, and the fuel tanks were not shielded, which made us very vulnerable to being set on fire if we were hit. We wore no parachutes until late in the war. . . . We flew two planes at a time to the target. The first attracted all the searchlights and antiaircraft guns, and the other would glide in over the target, with its engine idling so the Germans couldn't hear it, and bomb the target. With all the attention on the first plane, the second would make a successful attack.

Combat Misery

Many who fought in World War II knew intense misery. Their greatest American chronicler was Ernie Pyle, a reporter whose stories appeared in hundreds of newspapers. In North Africa in the spring of 1943, Pyle wrote this description of the ordinary men, without names, who had just won a battle, men not behaving like victorious heroes, but men clearly heroic.

A narrow path wound like a ribbon over a hill miles away, down a long slope, across a creek, up a slope, and over another hill. All along the length of that ribbon there was a thin line of men. For four days and nights they had fought hard, eaten little, washed none, and slept hardly at all. Their nights had been violent with attack, fright, butchery, their days sleepless and miserable with the crash of artillery.

The men were walking. They were fifty feet apart for dispersal. Their walk was slow, for they were dead weary, as a person could tell even when looking at them from behind. Every line and sag of their bodies spoke their inhuman exhaustion. On their shoulders and backs they carried heavy steel tripods, machine-gun barrels, leaden boxes of ammunition. Their feet seemed to sink into the ground from the overload they were bearing.

They didn't slouch. It was the terrible deliberation of each step that spelled out their appalling tiredness. Their faces were black and unshaved. They were young men, but the grime and whiskers and exhaustion made them look middle-aged. In their eyes as they passed was no hatred, no excitement, no despair, no tonic of their victory—there was just the simple expression of being there as if they had been there doing that forever, and nothing else.

Some of the greatest misery for soldiers occurred on the Eastern Front, where the Soviet Union's Red Army met the Nazi invasion that began in June 1941. The Germans made fast progress in summer, but winter cold and fierce Soviet resistance slowed them. A young German recruit captured war's misery in his diary in December 1941.

When will they at last pull us out of the line? . . . What is all this for? . . . When will we ever get back home? . . . With an empty belly almost everyone is suffering from dysentery! We feel weak and as miserable as dogs. Add to this the terrible cold. The frostbite in my

I'm used to the men going over every minute on the line. If you only knew what combat does to these boys—not in the physical sense, although that's bad enough—but mentally.

—American Red Cross Captain Liz Richardson, letter to her parents, May 28, 1945

Cold rations are distributed to American combat soldiers in Belgium in the extremely harsh winter of 1945. These young GIs do not bother to smile for the camera or lay down their weapons as they hold their mess kits and wait.

feet is growing ever larger and more infected with abscess every day. . . . And there are the Bolsheviks! . . . We cannot halt them.

Alexander Werth spent four years in wartime Russia as a reporter for the *Times* of London. Fluent in Russian, Werth talked often with ordinary people. One was a soldier, named Misha, a veteran of hard fighting against the Germans. Werth recorded this soldier's gripes in his diary on December 4, 1942.

"What we soldiers are interested in above all else," said Misha, "are three things: a wash, food, and sleep. Nothing else matters much. We don't sing songs—only sometimes, usually under compulsion. Perhaps they do in the rear: but we front-liners aren't interested in songs. It isn't what you people in Moscow imagine. We aren't interested in women either—not much. Oh, yes there are girls at the front—girls serving in canteens, and typists, and all that. But they won't look at anything below the rank of Lieutenant-Colonel—not they!

Misha's resentment of officer privileges was common among ordinary soldiers in all armies.

"Oh, I know, these people also do their job, I suppose it's just the old antagonism between the front and the rear. It's always existed; you can't help it. Take, for instance, our general. Some of us went to see him about an important matter. A young and pretty blond came out: 'No,' she said, 'you can't go straight in; the General is still resting.' (You never say of a superior he's sleeping; you must always say 'resting.') 'You will have to wait till I announce you.' 'And who are you, miss?' we said. 'I'm the typist,' she said. The General was, of course, sleeping comfortably in a real bed."

But there was no mistake about the goal.

"Our one aim now . . . is to get to Germany to give them what's coming to them. Last year we still used to give cigarettes to some miserable shivering Fritzes but not now."

The heat and jungles of the South Pacific also brought misery. Ogawa Tamotsu was a medic in the Japanese army. In an oral history interview forty-five years after the war he remembered the suffering.

I was on New Britain for three years, and here's what I learned: Men killed in combat are a very small part of those who die in war. Men died of starvation, all kinds of disease. They just fell out, one after another while on the run in the jungle. Amoebic dysentery, malaria, malnutrition. The ones without arms or with only one leg had to walk on their

---

T he tears of women and children are boiling in my heart. Hitler the murderer and his hordes shall pay for these tears with their wolfish blood; for the avenger's hatred knows no mercy.

—Russian poet Alexei Surkov, prose poem, "A Soldier's Oath," 1941

Fritzes

Nicknames for German enemy soldiers included Fritzes, Krauts, and Jerries.

own. Worms and maggots dropped from their tattered, blood-soaked uniforms. Men suffering from dysentery walked naked, with leaves, not toilet paper, hanging from their buttocks. Malaria patients staggered along with temperature as high as 103. It was a hell march.

For the ground soldier there was the constant chore of digging in, remembered by U.S. Marine veteran William Manchester in his memoir.

At the end of the day's movements, no matter how weary you were, you dug a foxhole, usually with a buddy. I struck big rocks and thick roots with discouraging frequency, but I never broke out my canned C rations (usually beans) or boxed K rations (cheese, crackers, ersatz lemonade powder, and "Fleetwood" cigarettes, a brand never heard of before or since) until I had a good hole. There was no hot food if you were on the line; fires were naturally forbidden. Most of us carried cigarette lighters. . . . If you were careful you could light a butt without drawing fire. Sometimes you could get away with heating soup or coffee in a canteen cup over a "hot box," a square of paraffin.

And there was boredom. Food in the U.S. Navy was better than canned C rations, but the vast Pacific disoriented sailors such as William McClain, who wrote an undated letter to his wife from the *USS Tabber*.

I'm leaving the date off this letter until I find out what date this is. I know it is Tuesday cause last night we had chicken salad for supper. We always have that on Monday cause we always have chicken on Sunday. I never know what day it is unless I think of how long it has been since we had chicken. The cook always seems to know.

Often thousands of miles from loved ones, soldiers treasured letters from home. But sometimes letters brought unhappy news. Russell Cartwright Stroup was a combat chaplain who dealt directly with the soldiers' worst physical and emotional wounds. Stroup wrote his family back in Lynchburg, Virginia, from New Guinea on November 26, 1944.

A boy visited me with a letter from his wife, who insisted, in a pathetic and apparently sincere letter, that she did love him, but that in a moment of weakness made up of loneliness and boredom she had slipped badly and was going to have a baby—not his. We had a long talk. He was angry and hurt and talked wildly. At last, though, I persuaded him to write to her that he would go right on helping her in every way until the baby came, and that neither she nor the baby would suffer. He also agreed that the baby could have his name: at first he violently objected, but I tried to show him how innocent the child was. Finally he said, "You know, that little fellow is just like me.

"Ya usin' two blankets or three?"

Bill Mauldin was perhaps the best-known American cartoonist of the war, especially among the soldiers whose misery he captured. His cartoons in the foot soldiers' favorite paper, the *Stars and Stripes*, were a must read.

Don't Sit Under the Apple Tree (1942)

Don't sit under the apple tree with anyone
      else but me
Anyone else but me, anyone else but me,
      no, no, no
Don't sit under the apple tree with anyone
      else but me
'Til I come marchin' home

> —The first lines of one of the most popular
> songs of the war years (written by Lew Brown,
> Charlie Tobias, and Sam H. Stept), testifying to
> many people's fears of separation

We both have to suffer for what isn't our fault." Then, more fiercely, "I ain't going to allow that kid to suffer any!" This was big of him, and wise. Later, he showed me his letter and it was a good one.

There are going to be lots of problems when the boys come home, and I have a world of sympathy for them and for the girls back there. I tried to help him see what his wife's life must have been with him away. War is a mess any way you look at it, and the by-products are worse than the direct consequences. No good can come out of such iniquity.

A Nazi propaganda leaflet air dropped over Americans GIs soon after the D-Day invasion attempted to build homesickness.

American soldiers!

She wanted to spend her life in peace and happiness by the side of her husband....

Now he will never come back!

Far away from his country and his people he was sacrificed for foreign interests on the battlefield.

HOW MANY AMERICAN WOMEN ARE

already **waiting in vain** for their husbands? How many mothers for their sons and how many girls for their sweethearts?

What about the girl you love? Will she belong tho those

WAITING IN VAIN?

SOURCE: 1944   AI - 031 - 2 - 44

The misery of combat reached back home to the families of those fighting. Loa Fergot was a student at Oshkosh State Teachers College in Wisconsin in October 1944 when she learned that her husband, Paul, a navigator on a B-24 bomber, was shot down over Italy. Almost fifty years later in an oral history interview she remembered waiting for news.

I got a telegram. It came to Neenah, my folks' house, and—I don't even know if I can talk about this. I was in school and it was between classes and I was standing by my locker, putting my books in, and I saw my folks walking down the hall. I knew right away what had happened, so—it was really tough, because I just slid down to the floor and sat there for a long time. And, of course, then my dad got down next to me, and he said, "He's only missing, you know, so there's lots of hope yet." . . . It wasn't until March [1945] that I found out that he was a prisoner, and from then on, I can remember, every day was beautiful.

I think the thing that affected us most, as students, was that the senior boys in the class ahead of us were already enlisting and leaving and by the time we graduated in 1943, between forty-five and fifty of the boys weren't in high school anymore.

—Marjorie Miley, Manitowoc, Wisconsin, oral history interview, 1992

Killing and Death

Men in combat saw death in all shapes and forms. Seldom was it the "clean" death portrayed to civilians on the home fronts. An American combat hero, Charles "Commando" Kelly, wrote about one death in his memoir published in 1944.

The next morning I went over to find out what had happened to the fellow in the other fox-hole, and when I pulled him out half his body remained behind. I began to feel things churning inside of me—which was bad, because it's better if you can close your mind to emotion. Picking up a shovel and covering what was left of him in the hole, I got hot and cold flashes. When the hot ones hit me, I was full of red rage. The cold ones took the heart out of me and drained away my confidence. I managed to beat the disheartened feeling down, but some of the rage stayed in me.

Ernie Pyle saw death all through Italy and France. When the European war was winding down, he forced his tired body off to the Pacific. On April 18, 1945, as he was reporting on the Battle of Okinawa, a Japanese sniper's bullet ended Pyle's life. A Navy man found on his body two handwritten sheets, with marked up and crossed out sentences—the beginning of a column that he never finished.

There are so many of the living who have burned into their brains forever the unnatural sight of cold dead men scattered over the hillsides and in the ditches along the high rows of hedge throughout

Wearing his helmet, Ernie Pyle peers out of a dugout shelter in Italy. Pyle was a journalist who got close to combat and to the soldiers doing the fighting. His understanding of American GIs combined with his superb writing skills to make him the nation's most admired war correspondent.

the world. Dead men by mass production—in one country after another—month after month and year after year. Dead men in winter and dead men in summer. Dead men in such familiar promiscuity that they become monotonous. Dead men in such monstrous infinity that you come almost to hate them. Those are the things that you at home need not even try to understand. To you at home they are columns of figures, or he is a near one who went away and just didn't come back. You didn't see him lying so grotesque and pasty beside the gravel road in France. We saw him. Saw him by the multiple thousands. That's the difference.

Among the highest losses were those of the Allied pilots who flew bombing raids over Europe. American poet and veteran Randall Jarrell captured war's brutality in his poem "Losses," published in 1945.

> In bombers named for girls, we burned
> The cities we had learned about in school—
> Till our lives wore out; our bodies lay among
> The people we had killed and never seen.
> When we lasted long enough they gave us
>   medals;
> When we died they said, "Our casualties were low."
> They said, "Here are the maps"; we burned
>   the cities.
>
> It was not dying—no, not ever dying;
> But the night I died I dreamed that I was dead,
> And the cities said to me: "Why are you dying?
> We are satisfied, if you are; but why did I die?"

Joan Hatfield lost her brother when his plane crashed over England on July 2, 1943; eight months later her boyfriend George died when his Lancaster bomber went down over Germany. On July 29, 1944, Joan, then serving in the British navy, wrote her parents.

Artist Stella Bowen sketched the very young Australian crew of a Lancaster bomber in April 1944 just before they left their English airfield on a mission. Soon after, she learned that their plane had gone down over Europe. Completing this oil painting, Bowen said, was "like painting ghosts."

Word cannot express how I hate this war, the parting from people, the loneliness that is always with you. The losing of people you love and who love you. Without even saying goodbye. Sometimes I feel so sad that I almost wish I were dead too. Seems a silly thing to say but death is so apparent here all the time.

Joan wrote again to her parents on August 26.

Why should any of these boys die, sometimes it seems to me that they are the lucky ones and that we who are left behind are the ones who are unhappy and lonely. Practically all my friends have gone now. . . .

Memories of death and fear stayed with veterans. In late 1944 Günter Grass was drafted into the German Waffen SS and trained as a tank gunner. Although wounded, he survived the war and in 1999 won the Noble Prize for Literature. Grass's best-known novel is *The Tin Drum* (1959), among the most searing portrayals of Nazi horror. In 2006, he published his memoir, *Peeling the Onion*, in which he admitted his wartime service and his "recurrent sense of shame." Sixty years later, Grass vividly recalled his first experience of combat, in 1945; he was seventeen years old.

A determined Nazi soldier throws a stick grenade during Germany's invasion of the Soviet Union in 1941. Sometimes called a "potato masher," this weapon could be thrown a long distance with deadly effect.

One can only assume that the encounter took place sometime in mid-April, when, after lengthy artillery bombardment, the Soviet armies had broken though the German lines along the Oder and Neisse [rivers] between Forst and Muskau to take revenge for their ravished land and millions of dead, to conquer, to triumph.

I see our Jagdpanthers, a few armored personnel carriers, several trucks, the field kitchen, and a thrown-together troop of infantrymen and tank gunners taking up position in a grove of young trees, either to launch a counteroffensive or form a line of defense.

Buds on the trees—birches among others. The sun giving warmth. The birds chirping. We wait, half drowsing. Someone no older than I am is playing a harmonica. A private lathers up, starts shaving. And then, out of the blue—or was the birds' sudden silence a loud enough warning?—a Stalin organ overhead.

There is no time to wonder where the expression comes from. Is it the way it howls, hisses, and whines? Two or three rocket launchers blanket the grove. They are ruthlessly thorough, mowing down whatever cover the young trees might promise. There is no place to hide, or is there? For a simple gunner, at least.

Jagdpanthers
Jagdpanthers were German tanks.

Stalin organ
"Stalin organ" was the common term for the Soviet Katyusha multiple rocket launcher.

The Katyusha multiple rocket launchers caused not only death and destruction but also great fear. Günter Grass long remembered the way the weapon "howls, hisses, and whines."

I see myself doing as I was taught; crawling under one of the Jagdpanthers. . . . The organ goes on playing for what is more likely a three-minute eternity—scared to death, I piss my pants—and then silence.

Beside me chattering teeth.

No, the chattering had begun even before the organ had played its piece to the end, nor did it stop when the screams of the wounded overpowered all other noise.

Brief as the interval was, it was sufficient: my first lesson taught me how to fear. Fear took possession of me. When I crawled out from under the Jagdpanther, I was no longer crawling the crawl I had practiced. I see myself crawling through a churned-up forest floor of decomposed leaves, into which I pressed my face for as long as the Stalin organ set the tone; the smell of them clung to me long after.

Still wobbly on my feet, I was assaulted by images. The birches looked as if they had been broken over somebody's knee: the falling treetops had set off some of our explosives. There were bodies everywhere, one next to the other and one on top of the other, dead, still alive, writhing, impaled by branches, peppered with shell splinters. Many were in acrobatic contortions. Body parts were strewn around.

Isn't that the boy who'd been tootling away on the harmonica? And there's that private, his lather not yet dry. . . .

The survivors were either crawling here and there or, like me, rooted to the spot. Some wailed, though not wounded. I made not a sound; I just stood there in my piss-soaked pants, staring at the innards of a boy I have been shooting the breeze with. Death seemed to have shrunk his round face.

Atrocity, War Crimes, Limitlessness

Armies on the Western Front tended to follow the rules of war. There were exceptions, however. The SS was an elite Nazi unit with a reputation for loyalty to Hitler and for brutality. Near the small Belgian town of Malmedy on December 17, 1944, an SS unit captured 150 American soldiers and herded the prisoners into a field. One who survived, Pfc. Homer D. Ford, told his story of the Malmedy Massacre in *Yank* magazine a month later.

The bodies of Americans massacred at Malmedy in December 1944 lie in the snow. Near this Belgium town, the Germans shot in cold blood nearly 150 captured American prisoners. The Malmedy Massacre became one of the most remembered brutalities committed against American soldiers.

They started to spray us with machine-gun fire, pistols and everything. Everybody hit the ground. Then as the vehicles came along they let loose with a burst of machine gun fire at us. . . . Then they came along with pistols and rifles and shot some that were breathing and hit others on the head with their rifle butts. I was hit in the arm and of the four men who escaped with me, one had been shot in the cheek, one was hit in the stomach and another in the legs.

Men were all laying around moaning and crying. When the Germans came over they would say "Is he breathing?" and would either hit them in the face with a butt of a gun or shoot them.

On the Western Front murder of prisoners was unusual. On the Eastern Front the Soviet Red Army and the Germans often murdered prisoners of war.

The Nazis also rounded up Jewish men, women, and children and early on began deliberately murdering them as part of the Third Reich's racial policy. Heinrich Bocholt was the pseudonym of a Hamburg policeman whose testimony a West German court investigator recorded in the 1960s. Sent with his battalion to Poland to murder Jews, Bocholt recalled how on November 3, 1943, they marched thousands of Jews from the Majdanek concentration camp to their deaths in nearby trenches.

Everybody got pissed off. I just wanted to get down to Belgium and start killing Germans.

—GI Clayton Shepherd, recalling his response to the Malmedy Massacre

From my position I could now observe how the Jews were driven naked from the barracks by other members of our battalion. . . . The shooters of the execution commandos . . . sat on the edge of the graves directly in front of me. . . . Some distance behind each shooter stood several other . . . men who constantly kept the magazines of the submachine guns full and handed them to the shooter. A number of shooters were assigned to each grave. . . . The naked Jews were driven directly into the graves and forced to lie down quite precisely on top of those who had been shot before them. The shooter then fired off a burst at those prone victims. . . . How long the action lasted, I can no longer say with certainty. Presumably it lasted the entire day, because I remember that I was relieved once from my post. I can give no details about the number of victims, but there were an awful lot of them.

In Asia and the Pacific the war had its own barbarity. Marching with the Japanese invaders into China was Ogawa Masatsugu, who had played shortstop on his college baseball team before the war and who after the war became a literature professor. He told his story in a 1983 memoir.

We admire the Japs for their tenacious fighting spirit, but we despise them for their resemblance to human beings.

—Marine Captain Walter Goldsberry Jr., letter to his family, December 29, 1943

I never really killed anyone directly. I shot my rifle, so I might have hit somebody, but I never ran anyone through with my bayonet. In China, [Japanese] soldiers were forced to practice on prisoners, slashing and stabbing, as soon as they arrived for training. "Stab him," they'd order, indicating an unresisting prisoner. I didn't move. I just stood there. The platoon leader became enraged, but I just looked away, ignoring the order. I was beaten. I was the only one who didn't do it. The platoon leader showed them how, with vigor. "This is how you stab a person!" he said. He hit the man's skull and knocked him into a pit. "Now stab him!" They all rushed over and did it. I'm not saying I determined it good or bad through reason. I just couldn't take the thought of how it would feel, running a man through with my bayonet.

In combat between Japanese and Americans neither side took many prisoners. Few Japanese surrendered, not wanting the shame associated with surrender. And Americans were often unwilling to allow surrender. At the end of the bloody fighting on Tarawa in 1943, for example, there were 4,700 Japanese dead and only 17 Japanese prisoners of war.

One of the finest combat memoirs of the Pacific War was penned by a young Marine named Eugene Sledge, who left college in Alabama in 1943 to join up. In his memoir, published in 1981 from his battlefield notes, Sledge described the effort of another Marine at the Battle of Peleliu in 1944 to get prized gold teeth from a wounded Japanese soldier.

The Japanese's mouth glowed with huge gold-crowned teeth, and his captor wanted them. He put the point of his kabar [knife] on the base of a tooth and hit the handle with the palm of his hand. Because the Japanese was kicking his feet and thrashing about, the knife point glanced off the tooth and sank deeply into the victim's mouth. The Marine cursed him and with a slash cut his cheeks open to each ear. He put his foot on the sufferer's lower jaw and tried again. Blood poured out of the soldier's mouth. He made a gurgling noise and thrashed wildly. I shouted, "Put the man out of his misery." All I got for an answer was a cussing out. Another Marine ran up, put a bullet in the enemy soldier's brain, and ended his agony. The scavenger grumbled and continued extracting his prizes undisturbed.

Such was the incredible cruelty that decent men could commit when reduced to a brutish existence in their fight for survival amid the violent death, terror, tensions, fatigues, and filth that was the infantryman's war. Our code of conduct toward the enemy differed drastically from that prevailing back at the division CP [Command Post].

Japanese atrocities were widely known to Sledge and his fellow Marines, one reason they dreaded surrender to an enemy they regarded as fanatical. One of the most notorious cases of Japanese treatment of prisoners was in building the Burma-Thailand Railroad. Thousands of British, Dutch, Australian, and American prisoners and larger numbers of forced laborers from Southeast Asia suffered horribly. Tens of thousands died to build a railroad 260 miles through mountains and jungle.

I f you were taken alive as a prisoner you could never face your own family.

—Yamauchi Takeo, Japanese soldier captured on Saipan, 1944, oral history interview

E arly we would be rewarded for prisoners, later when the stockade was full and info not needed we killed them, as they did us.

—Mark Durley, Pacific War veteran, oral history interview

Some 60,000 Allied prisoners of the Japanese, along with 200,000 Asian laborers, were forced to build bridges on the Burma-Thailand Railroad in 1943. Starvation, disease, and brutality led to the death of some 100,000. The Oscar-winning 1957 film *Bridge on the River Kwai* captured some of their story.

One of the prisoners was Cyril Wild, a British officer who testified on September 10, 1946, at the Tokyo war crimes trials. He described work on one bridge in summer 1943.

Q: What was the work which was supposed to be done at this camp?

A: It consisted chiefly of building a high level, heavy timber bridge across a river gorge. Also, building the embankments and digging the cuttings and approaches to it. The timber we felled and moved ourselves.

Q: How many prisoners of war died over that job?

A: I should say that that bridge cost a thousand British lives.

Q: Did you see the working parties lined up to go out?

A: I did.

Q: Describe their condition.

A: Well, every morning the same scene was repeated. In the half light, about 200 men would be paraded in the mud. None of them had more than a pair of shorts to wear, and some had kilts made of sacking. Practically none of them had boots. Most of those who had not were suffering from swollen-red trench feet. . . .

Q: How were the working parties treated by the Japanese engineers?

A: They were driven from morning 'til night without pity.

Q: In what way?

A: With a stick, sometimes with lashes of wire.

CHAPTER *3*

Mobilizing for Total War

World War II grew to unprecedented scope and scale. Unlike most wars before and since it demanded the total mobilization of all people in each nation. Men had to fight or work for the war effort and for little else. So often did women and even children.

Armies needed weapons—guns, tanks, airplanes, ships—and much more. In this total war the nations that could provide their fighting forces with the best and largest quantity of weapons and supplies would have the greatest chance of victory. Thus, the war became a war of economic mobilization. Which side could more quickly and fully mobilize their nations' factories for war production? Which could make the most deadly weapons?

"Produce for victory" became the watchword of the home front in all nations at war. At the beginning of the war Allied production lagged behind the Axis enemy in quantity and quality. As the war continued the Axis nations were slow to develop mass production of tanks, planes, and ships. They struggled with access to raw materials, particularly oil. Allied weapons were not usually of highest quality, but the Allies learned to make weapons in immense quantities and eventually could more than hold their own.

War factories required workers. Each nation had a different solution to its labor needs. As a democratic nation, far from actual combat, the United States chose not to force its citizens to work.

Detroit made the last American cars of the war years in early 1942. There would be no 1943 Chevrolet or 1944 Ford. The auto factories turned instead to weapons. At the Ford Motor Company's Willow Run Plant a mile-long assembly line produced 8,500 B-24 bombers. Ford's chief of production, Charles Sorensen, boasted, "Bring the Germans and the Japs in to see it. Hell, they'd blow their brains out."

WOMEN OF BRITAIN
COME INTO THE FACTORIES
ASK AT ANY EMPLOYMENT EXCHANGE FOR ADVICE AND FULL DETAILS

With Hitler just across the English Channel, Great Britain moved aggressively to recruit women into the factories that would turn out the airplanes, as well as the ships, guns, and explosives, to stop him. The number of women working in British munitions industries more than quadrupled between 1939 and 1943.

This is a war of engines and octanes. I drink to the American auto industry and the American oil industry.

—Toast offered by Soviet leader Joseph Stalin at the Teheran Conference with Roosevelt and Churchill in late 1943

Many other nations drafted civilian workers as they did soldiers. Some discouraged women from working, others encouraged it, and some required it.

In the end victory came to the Allies in significant part because of their successful economic mobilization. In the Pacific, for example, each American soldier was supported by an average of four tons of supplies compared to only two pounds for each Japanese soldier. By 1943 the Allied nations were producing three times as many airplanes and tanks and four times as many heavy guns as the Axis. Without that achievement the course of the war would have been very different.

War Production

Because of their head start as aggressors the Axis nations began the war with advantages in fighting strength and preparedness. Japan's initial assets included the Japanese Zero fighter and its pilots, perhaps the best in the world. Sakai Saburo was credited with shooting down sixty-four enemy planes in China and the Pacific. Long after the war, in an oral history interview, this Zero Ace remembered success and failure.

America was at first startled at the appearance of the Zero. Yet they produced new, powerful fighters one after another to "Beat the Zero!" Japan couldn't produce new planes in any numbers since the country didn't have the industrial strength. More than ten upgrades of the Zero weren't enough.

Yet if I can speak openly, even in 1945, if I were gripping the stick of a Zero and soared into the sky, I could meet their Mustangs or Grumman Hellcats and shoot them down. The combination of the human pilot and the Zero fighter was its true fighting strength. When Japan started the war, the level of our pilots' skills was reasonably high, but within a year the average level declined sharply. Veteran pilots were killed, leaving us like a comb with missing teeth. The development of planes fell behind, and the training of pilots lagged. The skill of the American pilots far surpassed ours by war's end.

Allied leaders understood the demands of war production. In one of his radio fireside chats, on December 9, 1941, just two days after Pearl Harbor, President Franklin D. Roosevelt told the American people of the nation's new production plans.

We must be set to face a long war against crafty and powerful bandits. The attack at Pearl Harbor can be repeated at any one of many points, points in both oceans and along both our coast lines and against all the rest of the Hemisphere.

It will not only be a long war, it will be a hard war. That is the basis on which we now lay all our plans. That is the yardstick by which we measure what we shall need and demand; money, materials, doubled and quadrupled production—ever-increasing. The production must be not only for our own Army and Navy and air forces. It must reinforce the other armies and navies and air forces fighting the Nazis and the war lords of Japan throughout the Americas and throughout the world.

I have been working today on the subject of production. Your Government has decided on two broad policies.

The first is to speed up all existing production by working on a seven day week basis in every war industry, including the production of essential raw materials.

The second policy, now being put into form, is to rush additions to the capacity of production by building more new plants, by adding to old plants, and by using the many smaller plants for war needs.

Heavy industry in California grew rapidly as the state became a major location for war production. Dozens of noses of A-20 attack bombers reflect factory lights as women workers at Douglas Aircraft in Long Beach prepare them for assembly in 1942.

love it if we made it

Soviet industry was not as advanced as that of the United States or Germany, but it proved formidable. As the German army moved east into the Soviet Union in 1941 and 1942, Soviet factory managers took apart their machinery and shipped the pieces eastward to safety, as far as Siberia; rebuilt the factories; and began producing airplanes and tanks, soon in far larger numbers than Germany. The Soviet newspaper *Pravda*, on September 18, 1942, reported on one such factory that was moved to Sverdlovsk in the Urals.

Among the mountains and the pine forests there is spread out the beautiful capital of the Urals, Sverdlovsk. . . . Winter had already

The heroic feat of evacuation and restoration of industrial capacities during the war . . . meant as much for the country's destiny as the greatest battles of the war.

—Soviet Army Chief of Staff Georgi Zhukov, memoir

come when Sverdlovsk received Comrade Stalin's order to erect two buildings for the plant evacuated from the south. The trains packed with machinery and people were on the way. The war factory had to start production in its new home—and it had to do so in not more than a fortnight. Fourteen days, and not an hour more! It was then that the people of the Urals came to this spot with shovels, bars and pickaxes: students, typists, accountants, shop assistants, housewives, artists, teachers. The earth was like stone, frozen hard by our fierce Siberian frost. Axes and pickaxes could not break the stony soil. In the light of arc-lamps people hacked at the earth all night. They blew up the stones and the frozen earth, and they laid the foundations. . . . Their feet and hands were swollen with frostbite, but they did not leave work. Over the charts and blueprints, laid out on packing cases, the blizzard was raging. Hundreds of trucks kept rolling up with building materials. . . . On the twelfth day, into the new buildings with their glass roofs, the machinery, covered with hoar-frost, began to arrive. Braziers were kept alight to unfreeze the machine. . . . And two days later, the war factory began production.

Mobilizing Workers

Making the weapons of war required workers, millions of them. All governments urged their citizens into the factories. In a fireside chat on October 12, 1942, President Roosevelt explained what needed to be done.

There are many other things that we can do, and do immediately, to help meet this manpower problem.

The school authorities in all the states should work out plans to enable our high school students to take some time from their school year, to use their summer vacations, to help farmers raise and harvest their crops, or to work somewhere in the war industries. This does not mean closing schools and stopping education. It does mean giving older students a better opportunity to contribute their bit to the war effort. Such work will do no harm to the students.

People should do their work as near their homes as possible. We cannot afford to transport a single worker into an area where there is already a worker available to do the job.

In some communities, employers dislike to employ women. In others they are reluctant to hire Negroes. In still others, older men are not wanted. We can no longer afford to indulge such prejudices or practices.

To meet growing labor shortages, many countries forced women to register for work. Canada made its announcement in Canadian newspapers in the fall of 1942.

This is the toughest war of all time. We need not leave it to historians of the future to answer the question whether we are tough enough to meet this unprecedented challenge. We can give that answer now. The answer is "Yes."

—President Franklin Roosevelt, fireside chat, September 7, 1942

The women in the factories have well-cared for hands and hair and they wear, whenever possible, pretty shoes. They have not given up their necklaces nor their bracelets nor their lipsticks.

—A 1944 British recruitment pamphlet titled
Eve in Overalls, perhaps downplaying the dirt
and sweat of factory work

ТРАКТОР В ПОЛЕ—
ЧТО ТАНК В БОЮ!

This Soviet poster from 1942, with the words "A Tractor in the Field Is Worth a Tank in Battle," proclaims the importance of farm work and of women workers. The poster's calm, reassuring image ignores the wartime devastation that Hitler's armies were then creating in the Soviet Union.

Threatened by Nazi invasion, Britain began in April 1941 to register women for work. A government pamphlet of 1943 explained the procedure.

By October 3rd, 1942, all women between the ages of 18 and 45, a total of 9,000,000 had been registered. Women between 45–50 are now being registered.

Briefly the procedure under this Order is that women who are found on registration to be either unoccupied or engaged on work not of national importance are called for interview at the Labor Exchange of the Ministry of Labor and National Service and given the choice of entering one of a short list of vital wartime activities which include the Armed Forces, essential industry, civil defenses, the Land Army and nursing. If a woman expresses no choice the Government has the power under this Order to direct her into industry. Compulsion has been necessary in only 26,000 cases—3/10 of one per cent of those registered.

The same British pamphlet explained how the Women's Land Army helped increase food production.

Uniforms, consisting of fawn shirt, breeches, socks, green pullovers, heavy shoes and red and green armlets, are provided free by the Government. . . .

The Women's Land Army undertakes all kinds of agricultural work. The greatest demand has been for dairy workers, but tractor driving has proved popular and women have also been surprisingly successful in forestry and lumber work. An auxiliary force has been established to help farmers at time of seasonal stress and a part-time army—made up of office and factory workers as well as rural housewives—has been of great value in bringing in the crops.

Many women liked their new jobs. Rose Kaminski, the daughter of Polish immigrants, lived in Milwaukee. In 1943 she left her young daughter with a neighbor and went to work first in a machine shop and then in a munitions factory. In an oral history interview recorded fifty years later she remembered the joy of her war work and her first day in the factory, when a supervisor who was short of workers showed her and several other women around.

So, he took several of us and walked into the factory, and here was this great big ordnance plant with machines all lined up in rows and everything and great big gun barrels. They were making great big howitzer barrels for the guns. Overhead were the cranes, and he showed us what we'd have to do.

I thought, "Oh, is that what my father used to do?" I said, "I'd like to try and see if I could do it." He said, "Well, you just have to learn how to work the crane, and all you'd have to do is pick up these great big"—they're like grinders that would go in and thread the barrels of these big howitzers—"and you'd have to set them in and then you'd just have to sit and wait until all of this goes through a procedure before you would take and lift up this part and move the gun barrel onto a flatcar and it would go out." I thought, "Well, gee, that sounded pretty nice." He said, "We'll train you. It will take you three weeks and you'll be able to run a crane yourself."

Well, I was running one in three days. It just came to me; I loved it. There was no problem. It was not difficult, and here I thought "You can see the gun barrels. You know that it's part of the war." It wasn't like at the other place where you had piddly little pieces, and you didn't know where it belonged. This seemed like part of it. You were doing something. You were accomplishing something.

Germany and Japan were less willing than the Allies to recruit women, especially mothers, to work in factories. Both used forced labor from conquered lands. The Nazis forced millions of people from all over Europe to work in their factories. In addition to these forced laborers the Nazis also selected healthier inmates from concentration camps and death camps to work. Many did not survive.

In 1943 Primo Levi, a twenty-four old Italian Jewish chemist, was taken to Monowitz, Poland, part of the Auschwitz complex that included the Nazis' largest extermination camp. Partly because of his scientific knowledge, Levi was chosen not to die, but to work, to help building a factory to manufacture synthetic rubber. The book he published in 1947 about his life as a slave laborer, titled *Survival in Auschwitz*, is now regarded as one of the great Holocaust survivor accounts.

We are at Monowitz, near Auschwitz, in Upper Silesia, a region inhabited by both Poles and Germans. This camp is a work-camp, in German one says *Arbeitslager*; all the prisoners (there are about ten thousand) work in a factory which produces a type of rubber called Buna, so that the camp itself is called Buna.

Primo Levi offers a compelling description of the Buna.

I would lift like fifty pounds at a time all day long. This was a man's work—a man's job. Men's jobs is what I did. I had a lady's job to start with and they saw how strong I was—my big hands and feet—and they put me on a man's job because during the war there weren't many men around.

—Emma Martin, Tennessee factory worker, in oral history interview

also helps boost morale

Women in the war

WE CAN'T WIN WITHOUT THEM

A female war worker uses a heavy tool to assemble a bomb. The U.S. government's rationale for hiring women was usually based on wartime necessity rather than equal employment opportunity. The same was true for its arguments for hiring African Americans.

There is no need for our nation to labor-draft women just because America and Britain are doing so.

—Japanese Prime Minister Hideki Tojo, October 1943, as Japanese production fell further and further behind

The Buna is desperately and essentially opaque and grey. This huge entanglement of iron, concrete, mud and smoke is the negation of beauty. Its roads and buildings are named like us, by numbers or letters, not by weird and sinister names. Within its bounds not a blade of grass grows, and the soil is impregnated with the poisonous saps of coal and petroleum, and the only things alive are machines and slaves—and the former are more alive than the latter.

The Buna is as large as a city; beside the managers and German technicians, forty thousand foreigners work there, and fifteen to twenty languages are spoken. All the foreigners live in different Lagers [camps] which surround the Buna: the Lager of the English prisoners-of-war, the Lager of the Ukrainian women, the Lager of the French volunteers and others we do not know. Our Lager (Judenlager [Jewish camp], Vernichtungslager [extermination camp], Kazett [concentration camp]) by itself provides ten thousand workers who come from all the nations of Europe. We are the slaves of the slaves, whom all can give orders to, and our name is the number which we carry tattooed on our arm and sewn on our jacket.

The Carbide Tower, which rises in the middle of Buna and whose top is rarely visible in the fog, was built by us. Its bricks were called Ziegel, briques, tegula, cegli, kamenny, mutton, téglak, and they were cemented by hate: hate and discord, like the Tower of Babel, and it is this that we call it:—Babelturm, Bobelturm: and in it we hate the insane dream of grandeur of our masters, their contempt for God and men, for us men.

And today just as in the old fable, we all feel, and the Germans themselves feel, that a curse—not transcendent and divine, but inherent and historical—hangs over the insolent building based on the confusion of languages and erected in defiance of heaven like a stone oath.

A 1945 photograph shows the immense but now abandoned Buna factory complex in Poland, built by slave laborers, tens of thousand of whom died there or in the nearby Auschwitz extermination camp. Primo Levi was one of those who survived to write his classic memoir, *Survival in Auschwitz*.

As we will be told, the Buna factory, on which the Germans were busy for four years and of which countless of us suffered and died, never produced a pound of synthetic rubber.

Allied Success

A major indicator of Allied production was the successful landing on the Normandy beaches in 1944. When President Roosevelt addressed the American people on June 12, 1944, six days after D-Day, he was careful to praise not only the men in uniform then fighting in France but also all the workers who made the miracle of production happen. And he asked all to contribute financially toward victory.

Americans have all worked together to make this day possible.

The liberation forces now streaming across the Channel, and up the beaches and through the fields and the forests of France are using thousands and thousands of planes and ships and tanks and heavy guns. They are carrying with them many thousands of items needed for their dangerous, stupendous undertaking. There is a shortage of nothing—nothing! And this must continue.

What has been done in the United States since those days of 1940—when France fell—in raising and equipping and transporting our fighting forces, and in producing weapons and supplies for war, has been nothing short of a miracle. It was largely due to American teamwork—teamwork among capital and labor and agriculture, between the armed forces and the civilian economy—indeed among all of them.

And every one—every man or woman or child—who bought a War Bond helped—and helped mightily!

There are still many people in the United States who have not bought War Bonds, or who have not bought as many as they can afford. Everyone knows for himself whether he falls into that category or not. In some cases his neighbors know too. To the consciences of those people, this appeal by the President of the United States is very much in order.

For all of the things which we use in this war, everything we send to our fighting Allies, costs money—a lot of money. One sure way every man, woman and child can keep faith with those who have given, and are giving, their lives, is to provide the money which is needed to win the final victory.

I urge all Americans to buy War Bonds without stint. Swell the mighty chorus to bring us nearer to victory!

The longer the war lasted the more the Axis struggled to produce sufficient war materials. At war's end the Allies captured German Field Marshal Wilhelm Keitel, who they later executed as a war criminal. On June 27, 1945, a prison interrogator asked Keitel why the Germans had failed to turn back the Normandy invasion. A stenographer recorded Keitel's answer.

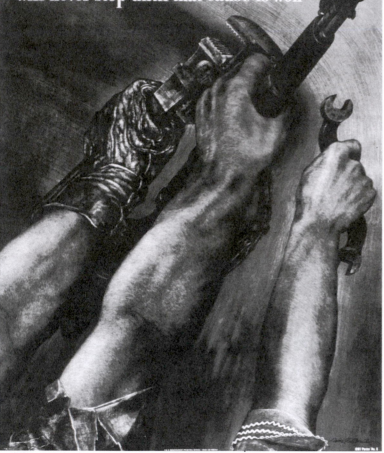

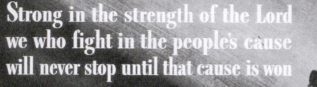

Strong in the strength of the Lord we who fight in the people's cause will never stop until that cause is won

A 1942 poster conveys in words and text the necessity for all Americans to work together. Three arms extend upward in unity. Each holds a tool of war—a rifle in the middle, wrenches on either side. The arm on the right appears to be that of a woman worker. Like many war posters, this one invokes religious belief and the theme of a "people's" cause—not a politician's or even a government's cause.

I am of the opinion that we were not able to compete with Anglo-Americans as far as the fighter and bomber aircraft were concerned. We had dropped back in technical achievements. We had not preserved our technical superiority. We did not have a fighter with a sufficient radius. As you know, we were on the way to make up this deficiency through new types, which did not make their appearance in time. I feel sure that the force as such, especially its personnel, officers, non-commissioned officers, and enlisted men, were not as courageous and anxious to fight as at the beginning of the war. I refuse to say that the Luftwaffe has deteriorated. I only feel that our means of fighting have not technically remained on the top.

Keitel also explained shortages of tanks.

The consumption of tanks on all fronts in Italy, Russia, and in the West was so large that the production could not compensate for the losses and sometimes, although the necessary tank replacement were available, they could not be transported to the front.

Economic might was measured not only in tanks and planes but also in food. GI Robert Easton wrote a letter from France on August 15, 1944, to his wife Jane in Los Angeles.

Have I mentioned the French, children and grownups, who come at mealtimes to eat what our men leave? When our boys finish, anything remaining is given to these hungry people. We feed a dozen or more at each meal. It is very pitiful—both the people and the fact we are so rich and never realize it. We eat, if anything, better here than at Camp Hood [Texas]. You would be astounded. Tonight we had pork chops, mashed potatoes and gravy, choice canned peas, bread and butter and strawberry jam, prunes and coffee. This morning we had grapefruit juice, absolutely divine pancakes made with powdered egg and milk, bacon and coffee with canned milk and sugar. The richness of all America is lavished here. You've no conception of the equipment alone. Today, for example, I saw a huge locomotive marked "U.S. Army" hauling a train of cars!

CHAPTER 4

Home Front Sacrifice and Morale

The destruction caused by the British and American bombing of Dresden in February 1945, was still apparent four years later, when this photograph was taken. The Dresden raid became one of the war's most controversial. Several decades later Henry Hatfield, an American radio propaganda producer during the war, commented: "Dresden is the one thing I'm really ashamed of. I mean hellishly sorry. We were behaving like the Nazis. The war was as good as over. It was an open city, full of refugees coming back from the eastern front. Who can say that wrecking this beautiful, nonmilitary city shortened the war?"

The hardship and sacrifice of World War II reached civilians on the home fronts of all nations. They had to do their part—working in factories, watching for air raids, saving and rationing items needed for military use. The war meant, for example, that there simply was not enough to eat. Many civilians suffered under the bombs that fell from enemy planes. And they endured restrictions on their freedoms, especially in the Axis nations but also in the democratic ones, including the United States.

Home front sacrifice was different in each nation. The hardships faced by ordinary people in the Soviet Union or Holland or Poland, for example, were horrendous. In comparison, America's burdens were light, as they were in Australia, Canada, and other nations more distant from the fighting. And yet Americans at the time and since sincerely believed that the necessities of war required them to sacrifice, to make do, to do their part.

If citizens were to endure hardship and danger, their leaders had to explain why sacrifice was necessary. The best leaders were masters at communicating to their people and answering the hard questions. Why must my family go hungry? Why are bombs falling on my city? Civilians on the home front had to know exactly how and why they were part of the war. They had to be convinced to do their part, and they had to have assurance that others were also sacrificing and that everyone was in this together. Maintaining civilian morale was a key necessity for victory. Even having fun during the war could be a necessity. Young couples continued to sing, dance, and fall in love.

This 1940 cartoon from a British newspaper, the *Daily Express,* shows Churchill as a bulldog facing across the English Channel, determined to stop the German invasion. The prime minister's public courage sometimes masked private doubts. After being cheered by people in the street, Churchill told a companion, "Poor people. They trust me, and I can give them nothing but disaster for quite a long time."

Forward Together

Few leaders in human history were more able to call forth sacrifice from a people than Winston Churchill. On May 13, 1940, three days after becoming British prime minister and with the German army racing toward Paris and the English Channel, Churchill spoke to the House of Commons. It was one among dozens of his great speeches.

I would say to the House, as I said to those who have joined this government: "I have nothing to offer but blood, toil, tears and sweat."

We have before us an ordeal of the most grievous kind. We have before us many, many long months of struggle and of suffering. You ask, what is our policy? I can say: It is to wage war, by sea, land and air, with all our might and with all the strength that God can give us; to wage war against a monstrous tyranny, never surpassed in the dark, lamentable catalogue of human crime. That is our policy. You ask, what is our aim? I can answer in one word: It is victory, victory at all costs, victory in spite of all terror, victory, however long and hard the road may be; for without victory, there is no survival. Let that be realised; no survival for the British Empire, no survival for all that the British Empire has stood for, no survival for the urge and impulse of the ages, that mankind will move forward towards its goal. But I take up my task with buoyancy and hope. I feel sure that our cause will not be suffered to fail among men. At this time I feel entitled to claim the aid of all, and I say, "Come then, let us go forward together with our united strength."

In the Soviet Union it was Joseph Stalin whose words mobilized the people. In a radio broadcast on July 3, 1941, as German armies drove into his country, he told the stark truth and demanded extreme measures from all citizens.

Comrades! Citizens! Brothers and sisters! Men of our army and navy! I am addressing you, my friends!

The perfidious military attack on our fatherland, begun on June 22nd by Hitler Germany, is continuing.

In spite of the heroic resistance of the Red Army, and although the enemy's finest divisions and finest air force units have already been smashed and have met their doom on the field of battle, the enemy continues to push forward, hurling fresh forces into the attack. . . .

By virtue of this war which has been forced upon us, our country has come to death-grips with its most malicious and most perfidious enemy—German fascism.

Our troops are fighting heroically against an enemy armed to the teeth with tanks and aircraft. Overcoming innumerable difficulties, the Red Army and Red Navy are self-sacrificingly disputing every inch of Soviet soil. The main forces of the Red Army are coming into action armed with thousands of tanks and airplanes. The men of the Red Army are displaying unexampled valor. Our resistance to the enemy is growing in strength and power.

Side by side with the Red Army, the entire Soviet people are rising in defense of our native land.

What is required to put an end to the danger hovering over our country, and what measures must be taken to smash the enemy?

Above all, it is essential that our people, the Soviet people, should understand the full immensity of the danger that threatens our country and should abandon all complacency, all heedlessness, all those moods of peaceful constructive work which were so natural before the war, but which are fatal today when war has fundamentally changed everything. . . .

All our work must be immediately reconstructed on a war footing, everything must be subordinated to the interests of the front and the task of organizing the demolition of the enemy.

The people of the Soviet Union now see that there is no taming of German fascism in its savage fury and hatred of our country, which has ensured all working people labor in freedom and prosperity.

The peoples of the Soviet Union must rise against the enemy and defend their rights and their land. The Red Army, Red Navy and all citizens of the Soviet Union must defend every inch of Soviet soil, must fight to the last drop of blood for our towns and villages, must display the daring initiative and intelligence that are inherent in our people.

People in the Soviet Union saw this poster in September 1941, when the Nazis were destroying everything they encountered in their advance eastward. The text at the bottom reads, "The Enemy shall not escape the people's revenge." Although the Germans have hanged a Soviet citizen and torched the house, this older couple will continue to fight. Their determined faces and the fist on the rifle make clear the thirst for revenge rather than surrender.

We must organize all-round assistance for the Red Army, ensure powerful reinforcements for its ranks and the supply of everything it requires, we must organize the rapid transport of troops and military freight and extensive aid to the wounded.

We must strengthen the Red Army's rear, subordinating all our work to this cause. All our industries must be got to work with greater intensity to produce more rifles, machine-guns, artillery, bullets, shells, airplanes. We must organize the guarding of factories, power-stations, telephonic and telegraphic communications and arrange effective air raid precautions in all localities.

We must wage a ruthless fight against all disorganizers of the rear, deserters, panic-mongers, rumor-mongers; we must exterminate spies, diversionists and enemy parachutists, rendering rapid aid in all this to our destroyer battalions.

We must bear in mind that the enemy is crafty, unscrupulous, experienced in deception and the dissemination of false rumors. We must reckon with all this and not fall victim to provocation.

All who by their panic-mongering and cowardice hinder the work of defense, no matter who they are, must be immediately haled before the military tribunal. In case of forced retreat of Red Army units, all rolling stock must be evacuated, the enemy must not be left a single engine, a single railway car, not a single pound of grain or a gallon of fuel.

The collective farmers must drive off all their cattle, and turn over their grain to the safe-keeping of state authorities for transportation to the rear. All valuable property, including non-ferrous metals, grain, and fuel which cannot be withdrawn, must be destroyed without fail.

In areas occupied by the enemy, guerrilla units, mounted and on foot, must be formed, diversionist groups must be organized to combat the enemy troops, to foment guerrilla warfare everywhere, to blow up bridges and roads, damage telephone and telegraph lines, set fire to forests, stores, transports. In the occupied regions conditions must be made unbearable for the enemy and all his accomplices. They must be hounded and annihilated at every step, and all their measures frustrated.

This war with fascist Germany cannot be considered an ordinary war. It is not only a war between two armies, it is also a great war of the entire Soviet people against the German fascist forces.

The aim of this national war in defense of our country against the fascist oppressors is not only elimination of the danger hanging over our country, but also aid to all European peoples groaning under the yoke of German fascism. . . .

Forward, to our victory!

Speaking on radio to Japanese schoolchildren on New Year's Day 1942, Prime Minister Tojo Hideki also presented his nation's cause in terms of good and evil.

You children must feel deeply grateful for the honor of having been born in the Great Japanese Empire, which is unparalleled in the world. The war we are fighting now is called the Greater East Asia War because it is the righteous war for constructing a glorious world of happy and peaceful nations by dispelling the evil forces of the United States and Britain, through the cooperation of Japan and the peoples of the Greater East Asia, who have been under their oppression for a long time. I hope you will heartily bear the glorious responsibility of Japan to accomplish this great cause.

Similar messages appeared in Hollywood films, where war images and stories captured large public attention. One of the most popular was *Mrs. Miniver* (1942). At the end a minister tells his congregation what the war means.

This is not only a war of soldiers in uniform. It is a war of the people, of *all* the people, and it must be fought not only on the battlefield but in the cities and the villages, in the factories and on the farms, in the home and in the heart of every man, woman, and child who loves freedom. . . . This is the People's war. It is our war. We are the fighters. Fight it then. Fight it with all that is in us. And may God defend the right.

Food and Rationing

Shortages of gasoline, tires, clothing, sugar, and meat caused sacrifice on the home fronts. Rather than a free market approach to scarcity, most nations adopted rationing and thereby sought to create an equality of sacrifice and a feeling that everyone was in the same boat.

President Franklin D. Roosevelt explained rationing to the American people in his message to Congress of April 27, 1942.

It is obviously fair that where there is not enough of any essential commodity to meet all civilian demands, those who can afford to pay more for the commodity should not be privileged over others who cannot. I am confident that as to many basic necessities of life

A fter Pearl Harbor I never played with dolls again.

—Jean Bartlett, who was twelve years old on December 7, 1941 rationing will not be necessary because we shall strive to the utmost to have an adequate supply. But where any important article becomes scarce, rationing is the democratic, equitable solution.

As the war continued governments rationed more food. An article in the magazine *Newsweek* on March 22, 1943, marked the first anniversary of American rationing with the title "Basic Diet Changes in View as Food Shortages Increase." The article reported also on the "black market," that is, Americans who sidestepped the law to buy or sell more than their share of meat by butchering cattle or hogs in secret.

Eager sixth-graders in a Washington, D.C., classroom learn how to use a new ration book. The government system of points and coupons could be confusing and frustrating, problems not conveyed in this photograph, which was likely designed for propaganda purposes.

A year ago this week, the Office of Price Administration set registration dates for War Ration Book No. 1 and thus launched America on its first venture in rationing. In the twelve months since, the country has added book No. 2 (with promise of Nos. 3 and 4 sometime this year); rationing controls have spread from one commodity, sugar, to more than 95 per cent of the nation's foodstuffs as well as shoes, tires, gasoline, etc.

America, too busy and far too harassed to mark the anniversary, was intent instead on a steady steam of new government food decrees.

Price Administrator Prentiss M. Brown announced that as of 12:01 A.M.. March 28, point rationing will cover meats, butter, cheese, canned fish, lard, shortening, margarine, and cooking and salad oils. For the first five weeks, each holder of Book No. 2 will have 16 points worth of red coupons a week to cover purchases of all these foods inclusively, thus permitting a national average weekly ration of 2 pounds "more or less" of meat (a half-point less than per capita consumption last year); 4 1/2 ounces of butter: 1 1/3 ounces of margarine (much less plentiful than butter); 4 ounces of lard; a little less than 2 ounces of cheese; and 3 ounces of shortening—in all, nearly twice as much meat and butter but only half as much cheese as the British are permitted. If he likes, however, the buyer can spend all his 16 points on butter, cheese, or meat alone. . . .

Despite all these rationing regulations, however, black markets still thrive. Even meat rationing estimates of 2 pounds of meat a week, Secretary of Agriculture Claude R. Wickard warned, depended on how effectively the government could stamp out the persistent evil whereby "every tree is an abattoir."

Jean Lechnir lived in Prairie du Chien, Wisconsin, during the war. She had two small children and was pregnant with a third when her husband was drafted in 1944. Nearly fifty years later she remembered rationing in a recorded oral history interview.

Everything was rationed when you come right down to it—anything that was worthwhile. . . . You had to wait in line to get butter or coffee and all us ladies that had husbands in the war—there were nine of us—we formed a card club. . . . When we played cards, the prize would be a pound of butter or a bag of sugar or a pound of coffee because we would hoard that. That's a horrible word to say—hoard. But we'd save our ration stamps and, of course, with our little babies and kids we didn't use a lot of coffee at times, not like we drink it now, and the butter was something else used very sparingly.

As troublesome as rationing was for Americans, it was far more difficult in other nations. Living in London during the war, writer Mollie Panter-Downes described rationing in an essay published in the *New Yorker* on August 10, 1941, four months before the United States entered the war.

The classic English topic of conversation, the weather, has vanished for the duration and now would be good for animated chat only in the event of a brisk Biblical shower—of oranges, cheese, cornflakes, and prunes instead of manna. Everyone talks about food. An astonishing amount of people's time is occupied by discussing ways and

Secretary of Agriculture Claude Wickard handles a plow to begin preparation of a new Victory Garden in Boston Common in April 1944. The image conveys the importance of growing food even in a public park designed for relaxation and beauty.

means of making rations go further, thinking up ingenious substitutes for unprocurable commodities, and trying to scrounge a little extra of whatever luxury one particularly yearns for. Nearly everybody now and then finds himself thinking of some kind of food to which in peacetime he never gave a second thought. Strong men, for instance, who normally wouldn't touch a piece of candy from one end of the year to the other now brood over the idea of milk chocolate with morbid passion. No matter how comparatively well one eats, deficiencies in diet lead to occasional empty moments which the individual mentally fills in to his own liking with filet mignon, plum-cake, or a dish of ham and eggs.

Horse-flesh is on sale, ostensibly for dogs, but possibly it appears incognito in many of the cooked foods which shops offer for human consumption. Eggs are rationed at the rate of one a week to a person. . . .

Now that marketing has become one long dialogue of queries and negative answers, the job of feeding a family is one which requires ingenuity, stamina, and endless time. The time factor has been sympathetically studied by the authorities in their drive to get women into line in the war industries. Some of the factories solve the problem by letting married women off for a couple of hours during the morning so that they can do their household shopping.

Mostly it was women who lined up for food, as was the case in front of a London fish shop. Even the legendary British patience for queuing was tested by wartime shortages.

A British government pamphlet published in 1943 described in detail the availability of various foods, including eggs and oranges.

Eggs. The number of eggs available for each ordinary consumer varies in different periods, but on an average is not more than about 40 eggs per consumer per year. Expectant and nursing mothers and certain classes of invalids are allowed additional supplies, the quantity varying with the supplies available. Distribution of dried eggs began on June 23, 1942: these can be bought from the retailer with whom the consumer is registered for shell eggs.

Oranges. Oranges are reserved for children under 5 for five days after the retailer receives his supplies. After five days, retailers may sell any surplus to the general public but are asked to reserve them for older children. Children under 5 use the tea coupons of the child's ration book (R.R.2) for oranges.

Life was much harder in the Soviet Union, above all in Leningrad. For 900 days, the Germans held siege to the city (today known as St. Petersburg), attempting to starve the people into surrender. Hundreds of thousands died, many of starvation. Valentina Fedorovna Kozlova was a teenager who survived. Fifty-five years later she wrote down her memories for David Glantz, a historian of the Battle for Leningrad.

First and foremost, the blockade meant hunger. I suffered from a state of extreme malnutrition. My prewar weight of 60 kilograms [132 pounds] fell to 39 kilograms [86 pounds] by July 1942. There was no running water or sewer system. Hunger dominated, and the winter of 1941–1942 was intensely cold. German bombers raided frequently. Buildings burned and collapsed, and people perished. There was no city transport. The first trams began operating in spring 1942.

I have many memories of the blockade. I have forgotten some things, but one can never forget the overall picture of that terrible time and no words can adequately convey the true nature of those things we had to live through. First there was the famine. One constantly wanted to eat. I dreamed (on the way to work on foot) of suddenly finding a box of fat or an entire horse lying around. Mamma helped our family somehow survive, except for Papa, who died on 30 March 1942 at the age of 62. Her wisdom and diligence arranged three square meals a day, even if it was hot water with some grain and cabbage and bits of bread. . . .

Gasoline was rationed nearly everywhere, including the United States. Americans had to place a ration sticker on their windshield. Most had only an A sticker, which gave them very small amounts of fuel. President Roosevelt explained the reasons for sacrifice in a fireside chat on July 28, 1943.

It is interesting for us to realize that every flying fortress that bombed harbor installations at, for example, Naples, bombed it from its base in North Africa, required 1,110 gallons of gasoline for each single mission, and that this is the equal of about 375 "A" ration tickets—enough gas to drive your car five times across this continent. You will

Doubtless President Roosevelt had in mind those like Valentina Fedorovna Kozlova when he chided the American people on their relative comfort in a radio fireside chat of July 28, 1943.

Those few Americans who grouse and complain about the inconveniences of life here in the United States should learn some lessons from the civilian populations of our Allies—Britain, and China, and Russia—and of all the lands occupied by our common enemies.

Please bring a bowl with a little rice. I am so hungry, I can't stand it.

—Mitsuko, Japanese sixth grader writing to her mother, August, 1944

Flying Fortress

The B-17 bomber, so named to suggest its power. It dropped more bombs in the war than any other American plane.

I could get an A sticker—that was about five gallons of gas a month, I think. It wasn't enough for you to blow your nose at.

—Ralph F. Dorris, American wartime teenager, in oral history interview

IS YOUR TRIP NECESSARY?

NEEDLESS TRAVEL
interferes with the War Effort
OFFICE OF DEFENSE TRANSPORTATION

The war brought a large increase in rail freight shipments and also passenger travel as soldiers, workers, businessmen, mothers, children, and other travelers scurried around the nation. The resulting congestion on the rails and crowded passenger cars caused the U.S. government to urge citizens to give up needless travel, just as they sacrificed in other areas.

better understand your part in the war—and what gasoline rationing means—if you multiply this by the gasoline needs of thousands of planes and hundreds of thousands of jeeps, and trucks and tanks that are now serving overseas. . . .

The longer this war goes on the clearer it becomes that no one can draw a blue pencil down the middle of a page and call one side "the fighting front" and the other side "the home front." For the two of them are inexorably tied together.

Every combat division, every naval task force, every squadron of fighting planes is dependent for its equipment and ammunition and fuel and food, as indeed it is for its manpower, dependent on the American people in civilian clothes in the offices and in the factories and on the farms at home.

Shortages of gasoline and the large numbers of people on the move to army bases and to new wartime jobs meant crowded trains across America. The hardships facing a traveling mother appeared in a 1944 U.S. government pamphlet titled *If Your Baby Must Travel in Wartime*.

Have you been on a train lately? The railroads have a hard job to do these days, one they are doing well. But before you decide on a trip with a baby, you should realize what a wartime train is like. So let's look into one.

This train is crowded. At every stop more people get on—more and still more. Soldiers and sailors on furlough, men on business trips, women—young and not so young—and babies, lots of them, mostly small.

The seats are full. People stand and jostle one another in the aisle. Mothers sit crowded into single seats with toddlers or with babies in their laps. Three sailors occupy space meant for two. A soldier sits on his tipped-up suitcase. A marine leans against the back of the seat. Some people stand in line for 2 hours waiting to get into the diner, some munch sandwiches obtained from the porter or taken out of a paper bag, some go hungry. And those who get to the diner will have had to push their way through five or six moving cars.

You will want to think twice before taking your baby into such a crowded, uncomfortable place as a train. And having thought twice, you'd better decide to stay home unless your trip is absolutely necessary.

But suppose you and the baby *must* travel. Well then, you will have to plan for the dozens of small but essential things incidental to traveling with a baby and equip yourself to handle them.

Bombing of Civilians

One hardship Americans did not endure was enemy tanks in their streets or airplanes overhead. Enemy bombing was a particularly hard fact of life and of death for many civilians as well as military men in World War II. Some doubted it was right to kill civilians, particularly women and children, to defeat the enemy. Some wondered whether bombing the enemy's cities increased chances of victory or instead made the people more determined to resist.

Japanese air raids in China offered some of the earliest indications of the effect of bombing. Peng Zigan, a twenty-four-year-old female reporter for the Chinese newspaper *Dagong bao*, filed this story of destruction in the city of Hanyang in the paper's August 12, 1938, edition.

"Nanzheng Street was hit," someone wailed. Those who had just returned from the bombed area were awash with grief and could not utter a word.

People streamed in and out of narrow Nanzheng Street. As in a funeral procession, many burst into tears. . . .

The section of Kuixin Lane from No. 23 to No. 36 was totally demolished by bombs. This was what the Japanese did best: in the twinkling of an eye, houses and lives were reduced to nothing. In many instances the entire family was lost, so no relative remained to mourn the dead. Rescuers had no choice but to put their house number plate atop their coffins to identify the victims. A certain Yang Xindan, who was both the leader of the street section and a rescuer himself, was killed. His mother, dumbstruck, used a fan to cool off the body, which lay quietly on a bamboo bed, as if he could still feel the heat. . . .

A section of house near the bank of the river was leveled. I was told that there were many people gathered at the ferry. [Then suddenly] bombs and machine-gun fire rained down from above, killing almost one hundred people both on the dock and aboard the ferry.

In Britain the worst came with the Blitz—the intense bombing in 1940–1941 by the German Luftwaffe, known to the British as "Jerry." Approximately 43,000 British civilians died. Rose Maccaulay was a writer working in the ambulance service in London. She described in

Martha Gellhorn reported the war over a period of eight years and from twelve countries. In January, 1941, she wrote from a city in China under Japanese bombardment.

Half a million people live in Kunming. When the air-raid warning sounds, they rush from the town without even locking up behind them. There are no bomb shelters in the city and no protection of any kind in these flimsy buildings, and there are no anti-aircraft guns.

The text for this 1938 cartoon by Feng Zikai, one of China's finest artists, reads: "I want to become an angel, / Soaring high in the sky, / Following the enemy planes, / And grabbing their bombs." Feng was a patriot active in resisting Japanese invaders. But, as this cartoon suggests, he was less interested in vengeance against the Japanese aggressor than in simply stopping the violence of war.

A secret British government report of August 31, 1940, described, in shorthand language, some of the consequences of the Blitz.

Lack of sleep beginning to tell on people in all districts, showing itself in paleness and lassitude of children and irritability of grown-ups.... Shelters not designed for mass sleeping, and responsible people fear serious consequences of impaired health and possible epidemics. School . . . in South East London has few attendances because of broken nights and head teacher states that children who come are heavy eyed and white.

This Nazi children's book, which was part of a series titled War Booklets for German Youth, celebrates the 1940 German bombing of the English town of Coventry. This bombing killed 380 people and destroyed much of the city center, including a fourteenth-century cathedral—far from the glorious depiction of the event portrayed for German children.

vivid detail a small part of the Blitz in a magazine article published in October 1940.

Where an hour back two houses stood in this small street, there is a jumbled mountain of fallen masonry, rubble, the shattered debris of two crashed homes; beneath it lie jammed those who lived there; some of them call out, crying for rescue, others are dumb. Through the pits and craters in the rubbled mass the smell of gas seeps. Water floods the splintered street: a main has burst; dust liquefies into slimy mud. . . . Jerry zooms and drones about the sky, still pitching them down with long whistling whooshes and thundering crashes, while the guns bark like great dogs at his heels. The moonless sky, lanced with long, sliding, crossing shafts, is a-flare with golden oranges that pitch and burst and are lost among the stars. Deep within its home a baby whimpers, and its mother faintly moans "My baby. Oh, my poor baby. Oh, my baby. Get us out." The rescue squad call back. "All right, my dear. We'll be with you in ten minutes now." They say it at intervals for ten hours.

Air raids disrupted the lives of survivors, including children, many of whom were evacuated from target cities to rural areas. A British government pamphlet published in April 1944 focused on increases in juvenile crime, setting this relatively small issue in context of the "abnormal" conditions of war, all with the rather cold language of government publications designed for opinion leaders.

Since abnormal home conditions are one root cause of juvenile delinquency, it is less surprising that figures have risen. . . .

(a) Evacuation

It is estimated that by the beginning of February 1941 more than 405,000, that is five out of six of the school-children usually living in the County of London, had been evacuated. Owing to phases of alternate alarm and quiet in the course of the war and for a variety of other reasons, there has also been a constant stream of return from reception to target areas, especially during the winter of 1939, and during the summers of 1941 and 1942. Some children moved four times in the first year of the war. The difficulties of making provision for their care at both ends were for a time almost insuperable. . . .

(b) Destruction of Homes in Target Areas

In England and Wales, as a whole, by November 1942, one dwelling house in every five had been damaged by air raids since the war began, and in some areas the figure was two or even three out of five. The London rate of damage was twice as great as that for the rest of the country. Children not only lost their homes, but ruined buildings gave endless opportunities for adventure and play which sometimes became rather wild. Toys, candies and innumerable other things attractive to children were buried under the rubble and remained there, sometimes for days, until the area could be cleared. It happened on occasion that children were brought before the courts for "looting," when they regarded what they had stolen as treasure-trove. It was, however, necessary to enforce regulations against looting strictly.

(c) Delinquency in Shelters

By September 1940 air-raid and rest-center problems began to be acute. By October 1941 more than a million people were practically living in shelters and many children were spending something like 15 out of every 24 hours in them, while those in industrial work were perhaps spending twelve. Many young workers gave up going home at all except at weekends. Hours for settling down for the night were too late for both children and adolescents. . . . Reports as to the amount of delinquency in shelters vary, but there is no doubt that these abnormal conditions contributed to its increase.

As Allied air power increased and Germany's decreased, raids against German cities got more and more destructive. The British-American bombings of Hamburg, a city in northern Germany, in late July and early August 1943 were among the most deadly of the war. Bombs from thousands of Allied airplanes created a massive firestorm that killed an estimated 44,000 civilians. The police chief of Hamburg filed his official report on December 1, 1943.

The reason for the damage being so serious and, above all, for the unusual number of deaths compared with previous raids, is the fact that firestorms developed. They, and in particular the one during the second major attack on the night of 27/8 July, created a situation

Nations under threat of bombing used posters to advise their citizens about blackout restrictions. This German poster appeared in 1944, when Allied bombs were destroying German cities. The message is simple and clear: The American bomber is death. Its bomb drops toward the light on the ground and toward the people in the house who have foolishly left a window shade open.

which must be described as novel and hitherto inconceivable in every respect. . . .

The horrific scenes which occurred in the area of the firestorm are indescribable. Children were torn from the hands of their parents by the tornado and whirled into the flames. People who thought they had saved themselves collapsed in a few minutes in the overwhelmingly destructive force of the heat. People who were fleeing had to make their way through the dead and the dying. The sick and frail had to be left behind by the rescuers since they themselves were in danger of burning. . . .

The streets were covered with hundreds of corpses. Mothers with their children, men, old people, burnt, charred, unscathed and clothed, naked and pale like wax dummies in a shop window, they lay in every position, quiet and peaceful, or tense with their death throes written in the expression on their faces. . . .

Posterity will only be able to maintain a respectful silence in the face of the fate of these innocents who fell victim to the bloodthirstiness of a sadistic enemy.

American bombers struck Tokyo on March 9–10, 1945. Soon after the war the United States Strategic Bombing Survey carefully studied the bomb damage in Tokyo and across Japan. In bland and quantitative military language, with frequent use of the passive voice, the survey team detailed its findings on July 1, 1946, under the simple title *Summary Report (Pacific War)*. The vantage point of this report is very different from the reports from ground level for London or Hamburg.

In the last year of the war American bombers destroyed most Japanese cities. In the Tokyo raids of March 1945, B-29 bombers dropped large numbers of incendiary bombs, and fires raged through a city of mostly wooden homes. About 90,000 people died.

On 9 March 1945, a basic revision in the method of B-29 attack was instituted. It was decided to bomb the four principal Japanese cities at night from altitudes averaging 7,000 feet. Japanese weakness in night fighters and antiaircraft made this program feasible. Incendiaries were used instead of high-explosive bombs and the lower altitude permitted a substantial increase in bomb load per plane. One thousand six hundred and sixty-seven tons of bombs were dropped on Tokyo in the first attack. The chosen areas were saturated. Fifteen square miles of Tokyo's most densely populated area were burned to the ground. The weight and intensity of this attack caught the Japanese by surprise. No subsequent urban area attack was equally destructive. Two days later, an attack of similar magnitude on Nagoya destroyed 2 square miles. In a period of 10 days starting 9 March, a total of 1,595 sorties delivered 9,373 tons of bombs against Tokyo, Nagoya, Osake, and Kobe destroying 31 square miles of those cities at a cost of 22 airplanes. The generally destructive effect of incendiary attacks against Japanese cities had been demonstrated. . . .

In the aggregate some 40 percent of the built-up area of the 66 cities attacked was destroyed. Approximately 30 percent of the entire urban population of Japan lost their homes and many of their possessions. The physical destruction of industrial plants subjected to high-explosive attacks was similarly impressive. The larger bomb loads of the B-29s permitted higher densities of bombs per acre in the plant area, and on the average somewhat heavier bombs were used. The destruction was generally more complete than in Germany. Plants specifically attacked with high explosive bombs were, however, limited in number. . . .

Total civilian casualties in Japan, as a result of 9 months of air attack, including those from the atomic bombs, were approximately 806,000. Of these, approximately 330,000 were fatalities. These casualties probably exceeded Japan's combat casualties which the Japanese estimate as having totaled approximately 780,000 during the entire war. The principal cause of civilian death or injury was burns. Of the total casualties approximately 185,000 were suffered in the initial attack on Tokyo of 9 March 1945.

Most leaders and their people regretted the loss of civilian life yet believed air raids to be a necessity of war. Victory required destroying factories, the homes of workers, the workers themselves, and enemy morale. But even at the time there were some who questioned. One was Katherine A. Hooper, the mother of an American pilot, who wrote to American General Henry H. "Hap" Arnold on May 3, 1943.

Last month my son Ted won his wings at Randolph Field. He is now going through a bombardment school, and in a short time expects to go to the front.

Japanese Children's Song, 1944
Air Raid. Air raid. Here comes an air raid!
Red! Red! Incendiary bomb!
Run! Run! Get mattress and sand!
Air Raid. Air raid. Here comes an Air raid!
Black! Black! Here come the bombs!
Cover your ears! Close your eyes!

It made a lot of sense to kill skilled workers by burning whole areas.

—An American Air Force officer who helped plan the air raids against Japan, in an interview after the war

Will you tell me—has he become what our enemies call him, "A Hooligan of the Air"? Is he expected to scatter death on men, women, children—to wreck churches and shrines—to be a slaughterer, not a fighting man?

Civil Liberties

The necessities of war often meant that citizens gave up rights and freedoms at home. In Japan and Nazi Germany there was no such thing as freedom of speech or of the press. Secret police watched everyone. Punishment was swift and hard.

In Munich, Germany, in 1942, Sophie Scholl and her brother Hans formed a small group of anti-Nazi university students called the White Rose. They intended to set off an uprising against Hitler. On February 18, 1943, the Gestapo (the secret police) caught the Scholls distributing anti-Nazi leaflets. The students had also painted slogans such as "Down with Hitler" on Munich buildings. Four days later Hans and Sophie Scholl were executed. These were some of the words in the pamphlet that led to their death.

Why do you allow these men who are in power to rob you step by step, openly and in secret, of one of your rights after another, until one day nothing, nothing at all will be left but a mechanistic state system presided over by criminals and drunks? Is your spirit already so crushed by abuse that you forget it is your right—or rather, your *moral duty*—to eliminate this system? But if a person no longer can summon the strength to demand his right, then it is absolutely certain that he will perish. We would deserve to be dispersed through the earth like dust before the wind if we do not muster our powers at this late hour and finally find the courage that up to now we have lacked. Do not hide your cowardice behind a cloak of expediency, for with every new day that you hesitate, failing to oppose this offspring of Hell, your guilt, as in a parabolic curve, grows higher and higher. . . .

National socialism must be attacked at every point, wherever it is open to attack. We must soon bring this rogue state to an end. A victory of fascist Germany in this war would have immeasurable, frightful consequences. Not military victory over Bolshevism must be the primary concern of Germans, but rather the defeat of the Nazis. This must be the *unconditional* first order of business.

The United States allowed its citizens more freedoms than the other major powers. Still, the government violated some civil liberties, the most troubling of which was the internment of Japanese Americans. In February 1942, the government ordered the roundup of Japanese Americans on the West Coast, fearing that some of them might engage in spying and sabotage in support of the enemy. In fact, there was not a single such case of disloyalty. Approximately two-thirds of the nearly 120,000 Japanese Americans rounded up were born in the United States and therefore were American citizens whose constitutional rights were severely violated.

One was Yoshiko Uchida, a student at the University of California, Berkeley. The government forced the Uchida family to leave behind most of their property (and their dog, Laddie) when it sent them to a camp in the Utah desert. Yoshiko Uchida describes their arrival in her 1982 memoir.

In the distance there were mountains rising above the valley with some majesty, but they were many miles away. The bus made a turn into the heart of the sun-drenched desert and there in the midst of nowhere were rows and rows of squat, tar-papered barracks sitting sullenly in the white, chalky sand. This was Topaz, the Central Utah Relocation Center, one of ten such camps located throughout the United States in equally barren and inaccessible areas. . . .

Testifying to their eagerness to be seen as American citizens, Japanese-American Boy Scouts conduct Memorial Day services at the internment camp in Manzanar, California. These Scouts may not have fully understood the irony of celebrating America's freedoms and ideals while interned behind barbed wire.

As the bus drew up to one of the barracks, I was surprised to hear band music. Marching toward us down the dusty road was the drum and bugle corps of the young Boy Scouts who had come with the advance contingent, carrying signs that read, "Welcome to Topaz—Your Camp." It was a touching sight to see them standing in the burning sun, covered with dust, and as they tried to ease the shock of our arrival at this desolate desert camp.

A few of our friends who had arrived earlier were also there to greet us. They tried hard to look cheerful, but their pathetic dust-covered appearance told us a great deal more than their brave words.

We went through the usual arrival procedure of registering, having a brief medical examination, and being assigned living quarters. Our family was assigned to Apartment C of Barrack 2 in Block 7, and from now on our address would be 7-2-C, Topaz, Utah. We discovered that our block was located in the northeast corner of the camp, just opposite the quarters of the Military Police and not far from the camp hospital.

The entire camp was divided into forty-two blocks, each containing twelve barracks constructed around a mess hall, a latrine-washroom, and a laundry. The camp was one mile square and eventually housed 8,000 residents, making it the fifth largest city in Utah. . . .

Each barrack was one hundred feet in length, and divided into six rooms for families of varying sizes. We were assigned to a room in the center, about twenty by eighteen feet, designed for occupancy by four people. When we stepped into our room it contained nothing but four army cots without mattresses. No inner sheetrock wall or ceilings had yet been installed, nor had the black pot-bellied stove that stood outside our door. Cracks were visible everywhere in the siding and around the windows, and although

In this cartoon, titled "Honorable Fifth Column" and dated February 13, 1942, Theodor Geisel, later known as Dr. Seuss, shows Japanese Americans from the West Coast lining up for explosives and waiting for the emperor to give the signal to attack the United States. In the months after Pearl Harbor, such images contributed to the erroneous conclusion that Japanese Americans were disloyal and that internment was a necessity of war.

our friends had swept out our room before we arrived, the dust was already seeping into it again from all sides. . . .

Daytime, with its debilitating heat and the stresses of camp life, was harsh and unkind, but early evenings after super was a peaceful time of day at Topaz. The sand retained the warmth of the sun, and the moon rose from behind dark mountains with the kind of clear brilliance seen only in a vast desert sky. We often took walks along the edge of camp, watching sunsets made spectacular by the dusty haze and waiting for the moon to rise in the darkening sky. It was one of the few things to look forward to in our life at Topaz.

Sometimes as we walked, we could hear the MPs [Military Police] singing in their quarters and then they seemed something more than the sentries who patrolled the barbed wire perimeters of our camp, and we realized they were lonely young boys far from home too. Still, they were on the other side of the fence, and they represented the Army we had come to fear and distrust. We never offered them our friendship, although at times they tried to talk to us.

Some white Americans saw that it was wrong to continue racial segregation at home while fighting a war for democracy abroad. Walter White, head of the National Association for the Advancement of Colored People (NAACP), told this story in his book *A Rising Wind*, published in 1945. The incident was one of the seeds that would blossom a decade later in the civil rights movement.

Three white American soldiers sat in front seats in a crowded bus in Florida one hot summer day in 1944. A wounded Negro veteran, wearing the service stripes of the Tunisian, Sicilian, and Italian campaigns, boarded the bus. One of the white soldiers got up and offered the Negro soldier his seat as there were no vacant seats. The bus driver told the veteran he could not sit in the seat but would have to move to the rear where Florida law provided Negroes must sit. The white solder pointed

The war made me live better, it really did. My sister always said that Hitler was the one that got us out of the white folks' kitchen.

—Fanny Christina Hill, an African-American aircraft factory worker in Los Angeles

One of the ironies of the war was the 442nd Regimental Combat Team, a segregated Japanese-American unit that served with great distinction in Europe. Some of its members had entered the army from the barbed wire internment camps. When President Truman awarded a presidential citation to the 442nd at this 1946 White House ceremony, he said: "You fought not only the enemy, but you fought prejudice, and you have won."

This drinking fountain was off limits to black workers at the Bethlehem-Fairfield shipyards in Baltimore, Maryland, in 1943. Even as they contributed to the war effort African Americans faced this kind of Jim Crow segregation

out to the driver that there were no vacant seats. The driver replied angrily that the Negro would have to go back anyway, as "niggers can't sit up front in Florida."

The white soldier turned to his buddies and asked, "Does he sit or doesn't he?"

"He does!" a roar assured him.

The white soldier turned again to the red-faced driver to tell him, "Either he sits down and you drive on or we'll throw you off the bus and I'll drive!"

The Negro veteran remained in his seat and the bus drove on.

Fun on the Home Fronts

Some citizens argued that the necessities of war required ending such frivolities as sports. President Roosevelt, a great baseball fan, disagreed in a letter written January 16, 1942, to the commissioner of baseball. As the president suggested, night games became common. Although many of the game's star players went into military uniform, baseball continued through the war.

My dear Judge Kennesaw M. Landis:

Thank you for yours of Jan. 14. As you will, of course, realize, the final decision about the baseball season must rest with you and the baseball club owners—so what I am going to say is solely a personal and not an official point of view.

I honestly feel that it would be best for the country to keep baseball going. There will be fewer people unemployed and everybody will work longer hours and harder than ever before.

And that means that they ought to have a chance for recreation and for taking their minds off their work even more than before.

Baseball provides a recreation which does not last over two hours or two hours and a half, and which can be got for very little cost. And, incidentally, I hope that night games can be extended because it gives an opportunity to the day shift to see a game occasionally.

As to the players themselves, I know you agree with me that individual players who are of active military or naval age should go, without question, into the services. Even if the actual quality of the teams is lowered by the greater use of older players, this will not dampen the popularity of the sport. Of course, if any individual has some particular aptitude in a trade or profession, he ought to serve the Government. That, however, is a matter which I know you can handle with complete justice.

Here is another way of looking at it—if 300 teams use 5,000 or 6,000 players, these players are a definite recreational asset to at least 20,000,000 of their fellow citizens—and that in my judgment is thoroughly worthwhile.

With every best wish,

Very sincerely yours,

Franklin D. Roosevelt

Some of the play of wartime looked forward to postwar peace and prosperity. This wartime ad for a German glue shows boys (not girls) at a play activity that will have future benefits. An English translation appears following the ad.

German children: Europe's future inventors!

While courageous men are fighting on the battlefields for the victory that will crown a happy and united Europe, the German home front is already working today on plans to benefit the freed peoples. The German youth is preparing for the great tasks of reconstruction and peace. They tinker and build models, engaging in guided and creative learning. Whether it is in shop class at school, evenings at home, or while participating in the youth organizations, UHU is everywhere. A special glue developed by the German firm Kunststoff-Chemie [Synthetic Chemicals], it is in demand as a dependable product.

War did not slow down romantic and sexual attractions. Quite the contrary. Connie Harris, a factory worker in Manchester, England, remembered, in an oral history interview in 1991, the special attraction of American GIs stationed in her country.

We had many a laugh as young girls with the Americans, I mean the Yanks were all over. You danced with them but you knew what kind of reputation you would get if you went out with Americans. There was one girl we called "Yankee Betty," it's a wonder she didn't catch something the way she carried on. Remember a lot of men were away. Let's face it, our lads in the army were not doing too badly with the German girls. It was more permissive during the war. It was wartime and you didn't know if you were going to die.

One complication in dating Yanks overseas was race. The American military segregated black GIs from white GIs. The British had their own racial problems, especially in the Empire, but they did not fully understand America's particular racial traditions, as General Dwight Eisenhower tried to explain in a letter to General A. D. Surles in Washington on September 10, 1942.

Here [in England] we have a very thickly populated country that is devoid of racial consciousness. They know nothing at all about the conventions and habits of polite society that have been developed in the U.S. in order to preserve a segregation in social activity without making the matter one of official or public notice. To most English people, including the village girls—even those of perfectly fine character—the negro soldier is just another man, rather fascinating because he is unique in their experience, a jolly good fellow and with money to spend. Our own white soldiers, seeing a girl walk down the street with a negro, frequently see themselves as protectors of the weaker sex and believe it necessary to intervene even to the extent of using force, to let her know what she's doing.

American GIs brought their swing music along with the jitterbug dance to England and then across Europe and Asia. To the Nazis swing was primary evidence of America's degenerate culture, one they believed had been created by subhuman Jews and African Americans. Still, Nazi leaders could not keep the music away from German teenagers. This report

They had no reserve about approaching girls in any way. They were just friendly and this was just completely new to us because we had always been brought up believing that people had to be introduced to you and all that sort of rubbish.

—Lola Taylor, an Australian wartime teenager, remembering the Yanks there in an oral history

issued by the Reich Ministry of Justice in early 1944 describes the problem of gangs known as "Swing Youth." In using the word "English" the Reich Ministry means the United States.

Even before the war boys and girls in Hamburg from the socially privileged classes joined groups wearing strikingly casual clothing and became fans of English music and dance. At the turn of the year 1939/40, the Flottbeck group organized dances which were attended by 5–600 young people and which were marked by an uninhibited indulgence in swing. After the ban on public dances they organized dances at home, which were marked above all by sexual promiscuity. The whole lifestyle of these members cost a considerable amount of money which they endeavored to procure through criminal acts and, in particular, through theft. The hunger for English dance music and for their own dance bands led to breaking in shops selling musical instruments. The greed to participate in what appeared to them to be stylish life in clubs, bars, cafés and house balls suppressed any positive attitude towards responding to the needs of the time. . . .

Partly as a result of the evacuation measures, these gangs have spread to other areas. Thus, for example, there was the Harlem Club in Frankfurt am Main, which held house balls of the worst kind. Even the youngest female members indulged in sexual intercourse with several partners consecutively. These parties were marked by alcoholic excesses at which people "swung" and "hotted."

Young American partygoers dance the new jitterbug. GIs carried the jitterbug around the world, along with American slang, dress, and food.

Wartime Posters Send the Message

People learned about the war through newspapers, books, magazines, radio broadcasts, films, and speeches. They also learned about it from tens of thousands of wartime posters. These documents sent strong messages and remain among the most interesting windows into the era.

Like most war propaganda, posters avoided confusing or ambiguous messages. Instead, posters were straightforward. There were no shades of gray. The world was divided in two factions, good and evil, and posters made very clear which was which and why. Words printed on posters were few and simple. Images were clear and direct and more important than the words. Designs were often colorful and catchy. A viewer walking by a poster could understand the message with a quick glance. Even a citizen unable to read could usually get the point. Posters appealed to emotions, often presenting war issues in very personal terms. This was your *war;* do your *part;* your *children will suffer if you don't.*

Governments, businesses, and other organizations established offices to support and oversee the work of poster making. They hired graphic artists, advertising executives, photographers, writers, and other experts to combine color, design, image, and words in the most effective way. The makers of wartime posters chose their images and words with care. They remained silent about controversial or disturbing information, such as conflicts among allies or differences among their own citizens.

World War II posters are worth more than a quick glance today. They offer an opportunity to speculate on the creativity, hard thinking, and emotional feelings necessary to create them.

An official of the U.S. Office of War Information wrote in August 1942: "We want to see posters on fences, on the walls of buildings, on village greens, on boards in front of the City Hall and the Post Office, in hotel lobbies, in the windows of vacant stores . . . shouting at people from unexpected places with all the urgency which this war demands." This poster, which hung inside Union Station, Washington, D.C., in December 1942, does just that.

"Ours . . . to Fight For"

In an address to Congress on January 6, 1941, before the United States had joined the war, President Roosevelt eloquently foresaw "a world founded upon four essential human freedoms." One of America's most popular artists, Norman Rockwell, turned the president's words into illustrations that appeared first in a popular magazine, the *Saturday Evening Post,* and then in poster format in 1943. In a concrete form familiar to ordinary Americans, Rockwell explained that they had to fight and sacrifice so that a man could stand and speak his mind at a town meeting; so that people could pray to their God; so that a family could expect the necessities of life, even a massive Thanksgiving turkey; and so that children could sleep in peace. Rockwell's simple images say nothing about the enemy, but they make clear nonetheless that only with the defeat of the Axis nations will these four freedoms be possible. Over four million copies of Rockwell's Four Freedoms posters hung in American public buildings and homes, making them among the most widely recognized images of the war years.

OURS...to fight for

Freedom of Speech   *Freedom of Worship*

Freedom from Want   *Freedom from Fear*

UNITED we are strong

UNITED we will win

"United We Are Strong"

Citizens needed to know not only their enemy but also their friends. This 1943 poster identified America's allies. The message is one of Allied unity. All the big guns point in the same direction and fire in unison. From this American perspective, however, not all allies are of equal importance. The flags in the foreground are Great Britain, the United States, China, and the Soviet Union, with lesser allies in background and hidden. The American flag and weapon are the largest of all.

"Attack on All Fronts"

This 1943 Canadian poster sends the message of unity. Soldier, factory worker, and woman—with machine gun, rivet gun, and hoe—all take a determined and aggressive pose in the same direction. The composition suggests that all three are important.

"The Spirit of Canada's Women"

Canada urged women to volunteer for military service. This poster offers as inspiration the medieval French heroine, Joan of Arc, a ghostly figure who rides on horseback with sword drawn. The uniformed women of the Canadian Women's Army Corps march in straight order.

"We Can Do It!"

The war effort needed women to take jobs not open to them in peacetime. Women who worked in shipyards and factories came to be called "Rosies," picking up on the title of a popular wartime song, "Rosie the Riveter." The "Rosie" image that became most popular was this one made by the Westinghouse Company. Rosie rolls up the sleeve of her work shirt, her arm flexed in a muscle pose, ready to go to hard labor. A bandana keeps her hair away from dangerous machinery. But this worker has not surrendered her feminine beauty: Her eyebrows are carefully made up, her lips are painted, and the finger of her left hand is finely manicured and polished. The contradictory message of strong, hard-driving factory worker mixes with traditional feminine beauty to reassure men and women that doing "man's work" will not turn women into men.

"Join the ATS"

Abram Games was one of Britain's greatest graphic artists. Games joined the army as a private at the beginning of the war, but the British government soon gave him ink rather than bullets. Of the dozens of war posters he designed, this one, made in August 1941, is among the best known. The purpose is to recruit British women to the Auxiliary Territorial Service (ATS) and to reassure them that women in military uniform need not look dowdy. Like Rosie, this British woman wore lipstick and has her eyebrows plucked and penciled. Known as the "Blond Bombshell," the image was too sexy and glamorous, some argued, and thus the poster was withdrawn from circulation and replaced by a more serious, businesslike image.

KEEP THESE HANDS OFF!

BUY the New VICTORY BONDS

"Keep These Hands Off!"

This Canadian poster encouraged purchase of defense bonds by showing the dark and taloned hands of Japan and Germany looming over an innocent mother and child. Other nations also used this theme of menace to women and children to depict the enemy's evil intentions. Implicit in such imagery was men's obligation to protect women and children.

CHINA FIRST TO FIGHT!

UNITED CHINA RELIEF
PARTICIPATING IN NATIONAL WAR FUND

"China First to Fight!"

It was possible to be confused about friends and enemies. Americans needed to know, for example, the difference between the Japanese and Chinese and to understand that the Chinese were the "good guys" in Asia. United China Relief, an organization that encouraged American assistance to China, prepared this poster to inform Americans that China had been fighting the Japanese long before Pearl Harbor. The Chinese soldier, mother, and daughter are all heroic and determined. They have suffered already, including wounds to the mother, but they fight on. The poster spares viewers the harsh brutality of Japanese conquest in China of the sort associated with the Rape of Nanking.

"This Is the Enemy"

Mobilizing the people required making quite clear that the enemy was wicked. This American poster shows a Nazi officer as the epitome of evil, his angular hat reinforced by his sharp nose, down-turned mouth, and sinister expression. The essential detail, however, is the hanged victim reflected in his dark monocle. The poster was a prize-winning entry in the National War Poster Competition held in 1943.

"Du Bist Front"

All nations had to convince citizens that their work on the home front was important to the actual fighting. The foreground of this German poster shows a muscular, bare-chested industrial worker (the idealized Aryan body type) wielding a large hammer. In the background is a helmeted German soldier, the beneficiary of his labor. The simple caption tells this worker, and all others, "*You* are the front."

"Jap Trap"

Posters often stereotyped the enemy. This was particularly the case of U.S. propaganda depicting the Japanese, here portrayed as a rat wearing thick glasses. The Douglas Aircraft Company made the poster to encourage its workers to conserve scarce materials in manufacturing airplanes and thereby help kill the rat.

Japanese Soldier

This Japanese poster presents a proud soldier, bayonet ready. He bears no resemblance to the rat or other American versions of Japan's fighting men. The text reads, "Let the victor look to the laces of his helmet." Like all soldiers, this one is being urged toward full commitment to victory, even to the details of his equipment.

"Above and Beyond the Call of Duty"

Citizens needed to put aside their own differences and unite behind their nation's cause. Race divided Americans. Most wartime posters showed only white Americans, but as the need for African-American soldiers and workers grew the government sought black heroes to serve as morale boosters. One was Dorie Miller, a messman on the *USS West Virginia* when it was attacked by the Japanese at Pearl Harbor. Miller's job was in the kitchen (the only place blacks could serve in the Navy), but he picked up a weapon and, at great risk to his own life, fired on attacking Japanese planes. This poster depicts a strong and courageous Miller, wearing the Navy Cross awarded him for his bravery at Pearl Harbor, with the burning ships in the background.

"We Will Raise the Flag of Victory over Berlin"

Posters encouraged sacrifice and fighting by holding out the promise of victory and peace. Made in 1944, the year before victory, this Soviet poster imagines the future when Soviet soldiers will march happily through Berlin's Brandenburg Gate. Flying on top of the capital city's historic landmark are the American, British, and Soviet flags, with the latter in the central position.

CHAPTER 6

Turning Points toward Allied Victory

At the start of the war the Axis powers had the advantage and pushed it hard. Germany soon occupied most of Europe and North Africa and threatened to conquer Britain and the Soviet Union. Japan advanced into China and southeast Asia and across the Pacific toward Australia. But the quick victory that the Axis nations hoped for was not to be. As the war continued the Allies built their economies and their armies.

By late 1942 there were signs that Axis hopes were fading. In the Pacific the battles of Midway and Guadalcanal caused some Japanese to sense that they had become victims of their own arrogance, of a "victory disease" that had caused them to underestimate the enemy's strength and will to fight. As the Americans and their allies gained control of the air and the seas in the Pacific, they began the bloody island hopping to Tarawa, Iwo Jima, and Okinawa, heading toward the Japanese home islands. Japan's desperation in the last months included sending off kamikaze pilots to deliberately crash their planes into enemy ships. It was a crude response at a time when the United States was beginning to test a new atomic weapon in the New Mexico desert.

In Europe the Soviets slowed, then stopped and turned back the German invaders. After its hard-won victories at Stalingrad, the Red Army drove toward the Nazi capital of Berlin. From the west, as German air defenses weakened, the Allies stepped up their bombing campaign. Finally, on June 6, 1944, Britain, the United States, and Canada opened a second front with a massive invasion across the English Channel and onto the French beaches at Normandy. They then pushed through France, across the Rhine, and into Germany, meeting up with their Soviet ally in April 1945.

The USS *Bunker Hill* was hit by two Japanese kamikazes near Okinawa on May 11, 1945, resulting in massive damage and loss of life. The Battle of Okinawa was the most costly of the Pacific War and included nearly 2,000 kamikaze attacks at sea as well as hard fighting on land.

One cannot bear the Germans. One cannot bear these fish-eyed oafs who are contemptuously snorting at everything Russian. . . . We cannot live as long as these grey-green slugs are alive. . . . Kill the Germans. Kill them all, and dig them into the earth. Then we can go to sleep. Then we can think again of life, and books, and girls, and happiness. But now we must fight like madmen, live like fanatics.

—Propaganda writer Ilya Ehrenburg, fueling anti-German hatred with these words in the Soviet Army newspaper, *Red Star*, August 13, 1942

Weary German soldiers seek shelter behind a wall during the Battle of Stalingrad in the fall of 1942. As winter set in and Soviet defenses hardened, the Germans' advance stopped. Stalingrad proved the turning point, after which the Red Army began pushing the Germans back toward Berlin.

Eastern Front

In summer 1942 the German army drove eastward, moving toward Stalingrad and the oil fields near the Caspian Sea. This was the Soviet Union's desperate "black summer." On July 28 Joseph Stalin issued Order No. 227, which became known as the "not a step back!" order. It was read aloud to all Soviet troops.

The enemy throws at the front new forces and, big losses notwithstanding, is penetrating deep into the Soviet Union, invading new regions, devastating and destroying our towns and villages, violating, robbing and killing the Soviet people. . . .

It is time to finish with retreat.

Not a step back! This must now be our chief slogan.

It is necessary to defend to the last drop of blood every position, every metre of Soviet territory, to cling on to every shred of Soviet earth and defend it to the utmost. . . .

Panickers and cowards must be eliminated on the spot.

Henceforth iron discipline is demanded of every commander, soldier and political worker—not a step back without orders from higher authorities.

To ensure iron discipline, Stalin ordered commanders to

organize within the army 3–5 well-armed blocking detachments (of up to 200 people each), place them in the immediate rear of wavering divisions, with the responsibility in the event of panic and disorderly retreat of the division's units, of executing on the spot panickers and cowards, thereby helping the honest soldiers of the division fulfill their duty to the motherland.

Soviet discipline, patriotism, military prowess, and good luck came to the fore at Stalingrad. Lasting from late summer 1942 until February 1943, the battle was marked by vicious street fighting and the first clear-cut Soviet victory of the war. Eventually the Red Army sent the Germans retreating, leaving behind about 100,000 dead and 110,000 prisoners. It was a major turning point of the war—some argue *the* major turning point.

Alexander Werth, a reporter for the *Times* of London, visited Stalingrad in February 1943, just a few days after the German surrender. Werth took careful notes of what he saw, which he used twenty years later to write his history of Russia and the war.

Everything around was strangely silent. The dead German with his leg blown off was still lying some distance away. We crossed the square and went into the yard of the large burned-out building of the Red Army House; and here one realised particularly clearly what the last days of Stalingrad had been to so many of the Germans. In the porch lay the skeleton of a horse, with only a few scraps of meat still clinging to its ribs. Then we came into the yard. Here lay more horses' skeletons and, to the right, there was an enormous horrible cesspool—fortunately frozen solid. . . . And, at the far end of the yard, beside the other cesspool, beyond a low stone wall, the yellow corpses of skinny Germans were piled up—men who had died in that basement—about a dozen wax-like dummies. . . .

This scene of filth and suffering in that yard of the Red Army House was my last glimpse of Stalingrad. I remembered the long anxious days of the summer of 1942, and the nights of the London blitz, and the photographs of Hitler, smirking as he stood on the step of the Madeleine in Paris, and the weary days of '38 and '39 when a jittery Europe would tune in to Berlin and hear Hitler's yells accompanied by the cannibal roar of the German mob. And there seemed a rough but divine justice in those frozen cesspools with their diarrhea, and those horses' bones, and those starved yellow corpses in the yard of the Red Army House in Stalingrad.

Defeat at Stalingrad was a serious blow to German hopes. On February 18, 1943, Nazi Propaganda Minister Joseph Goebbels delivered a radio broadcast intended to rally the nation. Goebbels explained that "total war" was absolutely necessary or the Bolshevists and Jews would destroy Germany and Europe. The official transcript of Goebbels's speech indicates in parenthesis the responses of the carefully selected Berlin audience and closes with the comment that "The minister's final words were lost in unending stormy applause."

What an example German soldiers have set in this great age! And what an obligation it puts on us all, particularly the entire German homeland! Stalingrad was and is fate's great alarm call to the German nation! A nation that has the strength to survive and overcome such a disaster, even to draw from it additional strength, is unbeatable. In my speech to you and the German people, I shall remember the heroes of Stalingrad, who put me and all of us under a deep obligation. . . .

The storm raging against our venerable continent from the steppes this winter overshadows all previous human and historical experience. The German army and its allies are the only possible defense. . . . Ten years of National Socialism have been enough

If Jerry were here with his whole army instead of facing Russia with most of it, we might be fighting till our hair is grey.

—GI Robert Easton, in a letter from Germany to his wife Jane, February 19, 1945

Despite Goebbels's rousing oratory, some German people began to doubt victory. A report of the Nazi Security Service in mid-1943 showed evidence of that doubt.

The telling of vulgar jokes detrimental to the state, even about the Fuhrer himself, has increased considerably since Stalingrad. In conversations in cafés, factories and other meeting places people tell each other the 'latest' political jokes and in many cases make no distinction between those with a harmless content and those which are clearly in opposition to the state. Even people who hardly know each other exchange jokes. They clearly assume that any joke can now be told without fear of sharp rebuff, let alone of being reported to the police.

to make plain to the German people the seriousness of the danger posed by Bolshevism from the East. Now one can understand why we spoke so often of the fight against Bolshevism at our Nuremberg party rallies. We raised our voices in warning to our German people and the world, hoping to awaken Western humanity from the paralysis of will and spirit into which it had fallen. We tried to open their eyes to the horrible danger from Eastern Bolshevism, which had subjected a nation of nearly 200 million people to the terror of the Jews and was preparing an aggressive war against Europe. . . .

We see Jewry as a direct threat to every nation. We do not care what other peoples do about the danger. What we do to defend ourselves is our own business, however, and we will not tolerate objections from others. Jewry is a contagious infection. Enemy nations may raise hypocritical protests against our measures against Jewry and cry crocodile tears, but that will not stop us from doing that which is necessary. Germany, in any event, has no intention of bowing before this threat, but rather intends to take the most radical measures, if necessary, in good time. (After this sentence, the chants of the audience prevent the minister from going on for several minutes.) . . .

Nazi propaganda minister Joseph Goebbels addresses a 1942 party rally in Berlin. The banner behind the dais reminds the audience, "Never forget that England forced the war on us." Goebbels was a superb orator, able to twist the truth as his German audience cheered and applauded.

The German nation is fighting for everything it has. We know that the German people are defending their holiest possessions: their families, women and children, the beautiful and untouched countryside, their cities and villages, their two thousand year old culture, everything indeed that makes life worth living. . . .

Total war is the demand of the hour. We must put an end to the bourgeois attitude that we have also seen in this war: Wash my back, but don't get me wet! (Every sentence is met with growing applause and agreement.) The danger facing us is enormous. The efforts we take to meet it must be just as enormous. The time has come to remove the kid gloves and use our fists. (A cry of elemental agreement rises. Chants from the galleries and seats testify to the full approval of the crowd.) We can no longer make only partial and careless use of the war potential at home and in the significant parts of Europe that we control. We must use our full resources, as quickly and thoroughly as it is organizationally and practically possible. Unnecessary concern is wholly out of place. The future of Europe hangs on our success in the East. We are ready to defend it. The German people are shedding their most valuable national blood in this battle. . . .

The total war effort has become a matter of the entire German people. No one has any excuse for ignoring its demands. . . . The people are willing to bear any burden, even the heaviest, to make any sacrifice, if it leads to the great goal of victory. (Lively applause.)

The Second Front

Although the bulk of the fighting in 1942 and 1943 occurred on the Eastern Front, the Allies did advance in northern Africa and then into Italy. Many Italians were increasingly unsupportive of their German allies and the war and eagerly embraced American GIs as they moved into their towns. John Steinbeck, a writer best known for his novel _The Grapes of Wrath_ (1939), was a war correspondent who sent this story back to the New York _Herald Tribune_ from Italy on October 14, 1943.

enormous

The pressure on the Italians must have been enormous. They seem to go to pieces emotionally when the war is really and truly over for them. Groups of them simply stand and cry—men, women, and children. They want desperately to do something for the troops and they haven't much to work with. Bottles of wine, flowers, any kind of little gift. They rush to the churches and pray, and then, being afraid to miss something, they rush back to watch more troops. The Italian soldiers in Italy respond instantly to an order to deliver their arms. They pile their rifles up in the streets so quickly that you have the idea they are greatly relieved to get the damned things out of their hands once for all.

An American Red Cross worker comforts an Italian child, one of the war's many orphans. An estimated thirteen million European children were without parents at the end of the war.

But whatever may have been true about the Fascist government, it is instantly obvious that the Italian little people were never our enemies. Whole towns could not put on such acts if they did not mean it.

The Soviet Union, where most of the fighting and dying was happening, wanted an invasion across the English Channel into France—a Second Front. The United States and Britain responded in 1943 that they did not yet have the military strength for a cross-channel invasion and that a premature one would be a disaster. After receiving this bad news an angry Stalin wrote Roosevelt on June 11, 1943.

Now, in May 1943, you and Mr. Churchill have decided to postpone the Anglo-American invasion of Western Europe until the spring of 1944. In other words, the opening of the second front in Western Europe, previously postponed from 1942 till 1943, is now being put off again, this time till the spring of 1944.

Your decision creates exceptional difficulties for the Soviet Union, which straining all its resources, for the past two years, has been engaged against the main forces of Germany and her satellites, and leaves the Soviet Army, which is fighting not only for its country, but also for its Allies, to do the job alone, almost single-handed, against an enemy that is still very strong and formidable.

Need I speak of the disheartening negative impression that this fresh postponement of the second front and the withholding from our Army, which has sacrificed so much, of the anticipated substantial support by the Anglo-American armies, will produce in the Soviet Union—both among the people and in the Army?

As for the Soviet Government, it cannot align itself with this decision, which, moreover, was adopted without its participation and without any attempt at a joint discussion of this highly important matter and which may gravely affect the subsequent course of the war.

General Dwight Eisenhower gives orders to American paratroopers ready to depart England for the jump into Normandy on June 6, 1944. One paratrooper, part of the pathfinders, the first group to jump, later recalled that "some of the pathfinders in the plane had their faces blackened. I did not put anything on my face. I felt if I was going to die, I wanted to die looking normal."

On June 6, 1944, British, Canadian, and American troops landed on the Normandy beaches of France. General Dwight D. Eisenhower, Supreme Allied Commander, sent this message of encouragement to the troops as they went into combat.

SUPREME HEADQUARTERS
ALLIED EXPEDITIONARY FORCE

Soldiers, Sailors and Airmen of the Allied Expeditionary Force!

You are about to embark upon the Great Crusade, toward which we have striven these many months. The eyes of the world are upon you. The hopes and prayers of liberty-loving people everywhere march with you. In company with our brave Allies and brothers-in-arms on other Fronts, you will bring about the destruction of the German war machine, the elimination of Nazi tyranny over the oppressed peoples of Europe, and security for ourselves in a free world.

Your task will not be an easy one. Your enemy is well trained, well equipped and battle-hardened. He will fight savagely.

But this is the year 1944 ! Much has happened since the Nazi triumphs of 1940-41. The United Nations have inflicted upon the Germans great defeats, in open battle, man-to-man. Our air offensive has seriously reduced their strength in the air and their capacity to wage war on the ground. Our Home Fronts have given us an overwhelming superiority in weapons and munitions of war, and placed at our disposal great reserves of trained fighting men. The tide has turned ! The free men of the world are marching together to Victory !

I have full confidence in your courage, devotion to duty and skill in battle. We will accept nothing less than full Victory !

Good Luck ! And let us all beseech the blessing of Almighty God upon this great and noble undertaking.

Dwight D Eisenhower

The day before the Normandy invasion, Eisenhower had hastily scribbled this message (mistakenly dating it July rather than June 5) on a pad of paper, to use as a press release in case of disaster. He intended to take full responsibility for defeat, including changing his original passive voice, "the troops have been withdrawn," to the active voice, "I have withdrawn the troops."

Eisenhower never had to use his D-Day "failure" message. On July 15, 1944, the German officer at Normandy, General Erwin Rommel, assessed the situation in a message to Hitler and recommended retreat.

As a result of the fierceness of the fighting, the extremely large amounts of materiel used by the enemy, particularly in terms of artillery and tanks, and the impact of the enemy air force which is in absolute control of the combat area, our own losses are so high they seriously reduce the operational effectiveness of our division.

Jesse Bobbitt was a paratrooper with the 101st Airborne Division. He landed in Normandy on D-Day, June 6, 1944. Sgt. Bobbitt survived Normandy but died in battle in Holland three months later. On July 4, 1944, he wrote his parents in a straightforward and bloodless style. Not only did military censorship restrict what a soldier could write home, but many soldiers did not want to upset family members with the details of combat.

Sorry I haven't written, but we have been pretty busy on this side of the pond.

I suppose the main questions are where am I, and how am I. I haven't got a scratch and at the present time I am behind a hedge-row in France. That is about all I can tell you as to my present location.

We have had quite a time since I have last written you. We were the first ones here so we got the hornet's nest all stirred up for everyone else. They had quite a nice reception waiting for us when we got here and things were really hot that first night and couple of days. The first day they threw everything but the kitchen sink at us and then they must have had a plumber take the sink out because I think they even threw it at us the second day. On the second night they jumped paratroops behind us and we got to pay them back for the reception they had for us.

One of our main troubles has been snipers. They hide in the trees and shoot at you, and you can't find them for love nor money. It was really tough on them when we did find them. A lot of them dress as French civilians and you don't know whom to shoot.

I think the prettiest sight I have ever seen was on the second day when some tanks came up to help us out. We were really in a touchy spot when they came, and that was the first of the beachhead we had seen and we were beginning to sweat those boys out. When we got the tanks we really went to town.

American soldiers land on the beach at Normandy on D-Day, June 6, 1944. They were among the 57,500 U.S. troops and 75,215 British and Canadians who would begin that day to drive the Germans out of France.

Although by the spring of 1945 the war in Europe seemed nearly won, deaths continued. New York University student Myra Strachner wrote frequently to her nineteen-year-old boyfriend, Bernie Staller, even after he was reported missing in action. On April 19, the day after she mailed him this love letter, she learned that he was dead.

Bronx, N.Y., April 18, 1945

Darling—

I was at your house tonight. They showed me some pictures of you taken in your high school class room and track team. The one I liked best was the one where you and another fellow were ready to start running. I looked at you, and this is what went thru my mind.

That hair is cropped close, but still is curled around my finger as if it were grasping it. I've kissed those lips. That expression I've seen so often. These legs were pressed against mine. I've held those wrists with my fingers. My hands have been in those hands. My fingers have touched those sides and both touched lightly and dug into those shoulders. My lips have kissed that throat.

And I know you had to be alive because you're so alive! Do you know what I mean?

Someday when we have long night hours before us, I'll tell you all about this—how I felt and what people said.

Today I cried again. I haven't since the day the president died. I was lying on my bed in the afternoon today and I found my lips forming the words, "It's too hard! It's too hard!" over and over again, and when I realized what I was saying I started to cry very quietly. Then I went into the den and played some of the songs that mean something to us and I cried hard for a little while. . . .

Darling, come to me in a dream tonight and tell me that you're alive and safe. Please! I know you want to tell me. Maybe somewhere in a prison camp tonight you're saying to your self that tonight you're going to try to tell me that you're alive. If there's anything good in this world, they'll let you tell me.

Now to sleep, and to wait for your message. I'll love you till I die.

Myra

As Franklin Roosevelt's funeral procession moves through Washington, D.C., April 14, 1945, citizens white and black show their grief over loss of the president who had led them through depression and the war. African Americans by this time had developed a special regard for Roosevelt, the first Democratic president to offer glimpses of racial justice and equality.

As the Allies moved into Germany they approached the city of Hamburg, where an eighteen-year-old named Erika welcomed them as liberators. In her diary on April 20, 1945, she wrote about her schoolmates, some of whom had been enthusiastic Nazis.

The liberators moved across Germany without meeting any serious resistance. Today they are in Nuremberg and in Czechoslovakia. In the meantime Vienna has fallen to the Russians. . . .

And now something else. The Nazi chieftains in my classes are behaving like shameful cowards. They had taken down the Adolf pictures and burned them and they are looking for something to replace the blank spaces on the wall. . . . Lisa K. is already burning all her party papers, documents of leadership service, etc., and she gets anxious whenever the girls under her still greet her with "Heil Hitler." And Gertrud B., who actually kept on believing in the good aspects of "Nazism," has woke up from her dreams and doesn't know what she should believe anymore. I stirred her up a bit by telling her a few things that could make her detest these criminals. In this way you can win over people we will need later.

Hopefully we will all survive the next few days. Things must be decided in any case. Boom, boom, boom. . . . You can hear the front, it's moving close—and we are waiting for what's going to happen. Waiting is the only thing that makes me nervous. . . .

On May 3, 1945, Erika made another excited diary entry.

At this moment British troops are marching into the city! At this moment the first state of freedom is beginning for us. *At this moment* the party is dead! *At this moment* the Nazis no longer have any power; the terror has stopped. Oh, I'm so excited. . . .

This happiness is still so new and unimaginable to me that I can't quite grasp it yet.—And there is such beautiful music on the radio! The Nazi music is finally gone once and for all, and Goebbels' speeches, which always really got on my nerves, are over and done with forever.

Many Germans fought to the bloody end. The Soviet army reached Berlin at the end of April 1945. With them was Vasily Grossman, a Russian war correspondent who had spent over a thousand hard days on the front lines. Grossman filled his war notebooks with telling details and poignant vignettes, which provided the raw material for the articles he wrote for Red Army newspapers. He hurriedly scribbled these notebook entries on May 2, 1945, as the fighting ended. After the war Grossman became a noted novelist.

The Day of Berlin's capitulation. It is difficult to describe it. A monstrous concentration of impressions. Fire and fires, smoke, smoke, smoke. Enormous crowds of [German] prisoners. Their faces are

The Third Reich is finished. Field Marshall Wilhelm Keitel signs the surrender document in Berlin on May 8, 1945, Adolf Hitler having committed suicide on April 29. Keitel was later tried and hanged by the Allies for crimes against humanity, including urging German civilians to murder downed Allied airmen they captured.

The *Queen Mary* arrives in New York on June 20, 1945, with thousands of troops returning from the European theater, happy to be home but worried that they might now be sent to fight in the Pacific.

full of drama. In many faces there's sadness, not only personal suffering, but also the suffering of a citizen. This overcast, cold and rainy day is undoubtedly the day of Germany's ruin. In smoke, among the ruins, in flames, amid hundreds of corpses in the streets.

Corpses squashed by tanks, squeezed out like tubes. Almost all of them are clutching grenades and sub-machine guns in their hands. They have been killed fighting. Most of the dead men are dressed in brown shirts. They were Party activists who defended the approaches to the Reichstag and the Reichschancellery.

Prisoners—policemen, officials, old men and next to them schoolboys, almost children. Many [of the prisoners] are walking with their wives, beautiful young women. Some of the women are laughing, trying to cheer up their husbands. A young soldier with two children, a boy and a girl. Another soldier falls down and can't get up again, he is crying. Civilians are kind to them, there's grief in their faces.

They are giving prisoners water and shovel bread into their hands.

A dead old woman is half sitting on a mattress by a front door, leaning her head against the wall. There's an expression of calm and sorrow on her face, she has died with this grief. A child's little legs in shoes and stockings are lying in the mud. It was a shell, apparently, or else a tank has run over her. (This was a girl.)

In the streets that are already peaceful, the ruins have been tidied. [German] women are sweeping sidewalks with brushes like those we use to sweep rooms.

The [enemy] offered to capitulate during the night over the radio. The general commanding the garrison gave the order. "Soldiers! Hitler, to whom you have given the oath, has committed suicide."

In addition to the loss of millions of lives, the war brought physical destruction visible in this image from a small town in western Germany in the spring of 1945. War correspondent Alan Moorehead wrote in April that many German towns had "no electric light or power or gas or running water, and no coherent system of government. Like ants in an ant-heap the people scurried over the ruins."

I've witnessed the last shots in Berlin. Groups of SS sitting in a building on the banks of the Spree [River], not far from the Reichstag, refused to surrender. Huge guns were blasting yellow, dagger-like fire at the building, and everything was swamped in stone dust and black smoke.

Reichstag. Huge, powerful. [Soviet] Soldiers are making bonfires in the hall. They rattle their mess tins and open cans of condensed milk with their bayonets. . . .

Optimists are learning English; pessimists are learning Russian.

—Berlin grim humor in the last weeks of the war, as people hoped the British or Americans would arrive before the Soviets, who they feared would be more vengeful

One of the most poignant wartime documents is a diary kept by an anonymous Berlin woman as the Red Army entered the city. In a long entry for April 27, 1945, she described the several rapes she suffered the previous day and concludes:

And now I'm sitting at our kitchen table. I've just refilled my pen, and am writing, writing, writing all this confusion out of my head and heart. Where will this end? What will become of us? I feel so slimy, I don't want to touch anything, least of all my own skin. What I'd give for a bath or at least some decent soap and plenty of water. That's it—enough of these fantasies.

It was in Germany, particularly here in Berlin, that our soldiers really started to ask themselves why did the Germans attack us so suddenly? Why did the Germans need this terrible and unfair war? Millions of our men have now seen the rich farms in East Prussia, the highly organized agriculture, the concrete sheds for livestock, spacious rooms, carpets, wardrobes full of clothes.

Millions of our soldiers have seen the well-built roads running from one village to another and German autobahns. . . . Our people have seen the villas of the rich bourgeoisie in Berlin, the unbelievable luxury of castles, estates and mansions. And thousands of soldiers repeat these angry questions when they look around them in Germany: "But why did they come to us? What did they want?"

Soviet vengeance and brutality extended to the rape of many German women. Alexander Werth, a reporter for an English newspaper, interviewed Soviet Marshal Sokolovsky on June 5, 1945, in Berlin. He later described their conversation in his memoir/history of the war.

When I mentioned the talk about Russian troops having run wild in Germany, Sokolovsky shrugged his soldiers. "Of course," he said, "a lot of nasty things happened. But what do you expect? *You* know what the Germans did to their Russian war prisoners, how they devastated our country, how they murdered and raped and looted. Have you seen Maidanek or Auschwitz? Every one of our soldiers lost dozens of his comrades. Every one of them had some personal score to settle with the Germans, and in the first flush of victory our fellows no doubt derived a certain satisfaction from making it hot for these *Herrenvolk* women. However, that state is over. We have now pretty well clamped down on that sort of thing—not that most German women are vestal virgins. Our main worry," he grinned, "is the awful spread of the clap among our troops."

The Pacific Theater

Early turning points in the Pacific came in great naval battles and then island hopping. Okinawa was the last battle, as things turned out, but it was the toughest battle of the Pacific War. Published in 1948, the official United States Army history of this battle in the Ryukyu archipelago included a table of losses. The precision of the table's numbers masks the

difficulty of counting the dead, especially the Japanese civilians. The initials "n.a." stand for "not available."

Comparative American and Enemy Major Losses in the Ryukyu Campaign, 1 April–30 June 1945		
Nature of Loss	American	Enemy
PERSONNEL		
Killed, Total	12,281	110,071
Army	4,582	n.a.
Marine	2,792	n.a.
Navy	4,907	n.a.
Captured	n.a.	7,041
AIRCRAFT		
Planes Lost, Total	763	7,830
Combat	458	4,155
Operational	305	2,655
Destroyed on Ground		1,020
SHIPS		
Sunk	36	16
Damaged	368	4

The few men like me who never got hit can claim with justification that we survived the abyss of war as fugitives from the law of averages.

—Marine Eugene Sledge describing Okinawa in his memoir

In his memoir of the Pacific War, *Goodbye, Darkness*, published in 1979, Marine William Manchester recalled the deaths on Okinawa and gave a few precious names to the cold numbers—first, a buddy named Chet and then others.

Back at battalion, the news of Chet's death deepened the section's numbness, but the days of cathartic grief, of incredulity and fury, were gone. One by one the Raggedy Ass Marines were disappearing. The Twenty-ninth was taking unprecedented casualties. On April 1 the regiment had landed 3,512 men, including rear echelon troops. Of these, 2,812 had fallen or would fall soon. The faces in the line companies became stranger and stranger as replacements were fed in. In our section we had already lost Lefty, of course, and Swifty; now Chet was done, too. Death had become a kind of epidemic. It seemed unlikely that any of us would leave the island in one piece. . . .

LST

LST and APA were naval designations for transport ships that carried men and equipment to invasion beachheads.

The happy dream is over. Tomorrow I will dive my plane into an enemy ship. I will cross the river into the other world taking some Yankees with me.

—Last letter home of kamikaze pilot
Araki Haruo, 1945

Lefty had been Harvard '45 and premed; Swifty had been Ohio State '44 and an engineering major; Chet, Colgate '45, hadn't picked a major; Wally, MIT '43, would have become a physicist.

Manchester himself was badly wounded in early June.

For four hours I was left for dead. Then one of our corpsmen, Doc Logan, found I was still hanging on. He gave me two shots of morphine and I was evacuated to an LST offshore which served as a clearing house for casualties. All the beautiful white hospital ships—*Solace, Relief,* and *Comfort*—were gone. There were just too many wounded men; they couldn't handle the casualty traffic. So I sailed off for Saipan on an APA. Goodbye Okinawa, and up yours.

Americans feared that the bloody Battle of Okinawa was prelude to what they would face invading the Japanese mainland. Araki Shigeko, widow of a kamikaze pilot who died in the Battle of Okinawa, remembered in an oral history interview her determination to fight on if the Americans invaded the Japanese mainland.

We were going to do it with our bamboo spears. When they landed we would attack them. We had those spears at our right hand at all times at the factory. "Each one, stab one, without fail!" they'd tell us. "Yes!" we'd reply in unison.

Our spear was about a meter and a half long, with a sharp point cut diagonally across at the end. We practiced every morning. "Thrust! Thrust! Thrust!" I thought I'd definitely be able to stab them. . . . It's amazing isn't it? Beyond comprehension today. At that time we had an unbounded faith in Japan. We felt the Yamato race was unequaled.

By summer 1945 the Americans wanted the war with Japan over as soon as possible and with as little loss of American life as possible. That consideration pushed the decision to use the new atomic bomb. Meeting with his British and Soviet counterparts at Potsdam, near Berlin, President Harry Truman learned that American scientists had successfully tested the new weapon. In his diary for July 25, 1945, he gave some of the reasons why he ordered its use. The debate over Truman's decision continues.

We have discovered the most terrible bomb in the history of the world. It may be the fire destruction prophesied in the Euphrates Valley era, after Noah and his fabulous ark. Anyway we think we have found the way to cause a disintegration of the atom. An experiment in the New Mexican desert was startling—to put it mildly. Thirteen pounds of the explosive caused the complete disintegration of a steel tower sixty feet high, created a crater six feet deep and twelve hundred feet in diameter, knocked over a steel tower a half mile away, and knocked men down ten thousand yards away. The explosion was visible for more than two hundred miles and audible for forty miles and more.

This weapon is to be used against Japan between now and August 10. I have told the secretary of war, Mr. [Henry] Stimson, to use it so that military objectives and soldiers and sailors are the target and not women and children. Even if the Japs are savages, ruthless, merciless and fanatic, we as the leader of the world for the common welfare cannot drop this terrible bomb on the old capital [Kyoto] or the new [Tokyo]. He and I are in accord. The target will be a purely military one and we will issue a warning statement asking the Japs to surrender and save lives. I'm sure they will not do that, but we will have given them the chance. It is certainly a good thing for the world that Hitler's crowd or Stalin's did not discover this atomic bomb. It seems to be the most terrible thing ever discovered, but it can be made the most useful.

Joe Rosenthal, an Associated Press photographer, took this image of the flag raising on Iwo Jima on February 23, 1945. It would become one of the most famous photographs of the war and the basis for the Iwo Jima Memorial outside Washington, D.C.

On August 6, 1945, the *Enola Gay*, an American B-29 bomber named for the pilot's mother, dropped an atomic bomb on the city of Hiroshima. About 80,000 people died. Suffering and death continued years later from radiation effects. Most fatalities were civilian, contrary to President Truman's Potsdam diary entry. On August 6 a White House press release informed the world of the new weapon and boasted of the scientific achievement of the top-secret Manhattan Project that had built it.

Sixteen hours ago an American airplane dropped one bomb on Hiroshima, an important Japanese Army base. That bomb had more power than 20,000 tons of T.N.T. It had more than two thousand times the blast power of the British "Grand Slam" which is the largest bomb ever yet used in the history of warfare.

Japanese

A column of smoke rises 60,000 feet over Nagasaki, after an American B-29 dropped the second atomic bomb on August 9, 1945. The blast killed about 74,000 people, including some 350 prisoners of war. In the years to come the debate over the necessity of a second bomb intensified.

The Japanese began the war from the air at Pearl Harbor. They have been repaid many fold. And the end is not yet. With this bomb we have now added a new and revolutionary increase in destruction to supplement the growing power of our armed forces. In their present form these bombs are now in production and even more powerful forms are in development.

It is an atomic bomb. It is a harnessing of the basic power of the universe. The force from which the sun draws its power has been loosed against those who brought war to the Far East.

Before 1939, it was the accepted belief of scientists that it was theoretically possible to release atomic energy. But no one knew any practical method of doing it. By 1942, however, we knew that the Germans were working feverishly to find a way to add atomic energy to the other engines of war with which they hoped to enslave the world. But they failed. We may be grateful to Providence that the Germans got the V-1's and V-2's late and in limited quantities and even more grateful that they did not get the atomic bomb at all.

The battle of the laboratories held fateful risks for us as well as the battles of the air, land and sea, and we have now won the battle of the laboratories as we have won the other battles. . . .

The greatest marvel is not the size of the enterprise, its secrecy, nor its cost, but the achievement of scientific brains in putting together infinitely complex pieces of knowledge held by many men in different fields of science into a workable plan. And hardly less marvelous has been the capacity of industry to design, and of labor to operate, the machines and methods to do things never done before so that the brain child of many minds came forth in physical shape and performed as it was supposed to do. Both science and industry worked under the direction of the United States Army, which achieved a unique success in managing so diverse a problem in the advancement of knowledge in an amazingly short time. It is doubtful if such another combination could be got together in the world. What has been done is the greatest achievement of organized science in history. It was done under high pressure and without failure.

After the Soviet Union declared war on Japan on August 8 and the United States dropped a second bomb, on Nagasaki on August 9, Japan surrendered. On August 15, the people of Japan gathered to listen to a radio broadcast from their emperor. They heard for the first time Hirohito's high-pitched voice, telling them the war was over. He never used the words "surrender" or "defeat." Nor did the emperor take responsibility for the war.

We declared war on America and Britain out of Our sincere desire to ensure Japan's self preservation and the stabilization of East Asia, it being far from Our thought either to infringe upon the sovereignty of other nations or to embark upon territorial aggrandizement. But now the war has lasted for nearly four years. Despite the best that has been done by everyone—the gallant fighting of military and naval forces, the diligence and assiduity of Our servants of the State and the devoted service of Our one hundred million people, the war situation has developed not necessarily to Japan's advantage, while the general trends of the world have all turned against her interest. Moreover, the enemy has begun to employ a new and most cruel bomb, the power of which to do damage is indeed incalculable, taking the toll of many innocent lives. Should We continue to fight, it would not only result in an ultimate collapse and obliteration of the Japanese nation, but also it would lead to the total extinction of human civilization. . . .

The hardship and suffering to which Our nation is to be subjected hereafter will be certainly great. We are keenly aware of the inmost feelings of all ye, Our subjects. However, it is according to the dictate of time and fate that We have resolved to pave the way for a grand peace for all the generations to come by enduring the unendurable and suffering what is insufferable.

The only one who wept at the actual news of Japan's defeat was the commander. I listened to the news, laughing. I was going to be able to return to Japan! I could hardly contain myself. I'd live!

—Ogawa Tamotsu, a Japanese medic in the South Pacific, remembering the end of the war, forty-five years later

There have been debates from the beginning over whether Japan would have surrendered without the two bombs, whether the bombs saved American lives by avoiding a costly invasion of the home islands, and what role atomic weapons played in the origins of the Cold War as demonstrations to the Soviet Union of America's new power. An early criticism came from an American Protestant church leader, Samuel Cavert, who sent a telegram to President Truman on August 9, 1945.

WB71 114 2 EXTRA   AUG 9 11 22 AM 1945

WUX NEWYORK NY AUG 9 1945 1046A

HONORABLE HARRY S TRUMAN

 PRESIDENT OF THE UNITED STATES THE WHITE HOUSE

MANY CHRISTIANS DEEPLY DISTURBED OVER USE OF ATOMIC BOMBS

AGAINST JAPANESE CITIES BECAUSE OF THEIR NECESSARILY

INDISCRIMINATE DESTRUCTIVE EFFORTS AND BECAUSE THEIR USE SETS

EXTREMELY DANGEROUS PRECEDENT FOR FUTURE OF MANKIND. BISHOP

OXNAM PRESIDENT OF THE COUNCIL AND JOHN FOSTER DULLES CHAIRMAN

OF ITS COMMISSION ON A JUST AND DURABLE PEACE ARE PREPARING

STATEMENT FOR PROBABLE RELEASE TOMORROW URGING THAT ATOMIC

BOMBS BE REGARDED AS TRUST FOR HUMANITY AND THAT JAPANESE

NATION BE GIVEN GENUINE OPPORTUNITY AND TIME TO VERIFY FACTS

ABOUT NEW BOMB AND TO ACCEPT SURRENDER TERMS. RESPECTFULLY

URGE THAT AMPLE OPPORTUNITY BE GIVEN JAPAN TO RECONSIDER

ULTIMATUM BEFORE ANY FURTHER DEVASTATION BY ATOMIC BOMB IS

VISITED UPON HER PEOPLE

 FEDERAL COUNCIL OF THE CHURCHES OF CHRIST IN AMERICA

 SAMUEL MCCREA CAVERT GENERAL SECRETARY.

The President responded, capturing the emotions of many in his generation.

692-A

August 11, 1945

My dear Mr. Cavert:

I appreciated very much your telegram of August ninth.

Nobody is more disturbed over the use of Atomic bombs than I am but I was greatly disturbed over the unwarranted attack by the Japanese on Pearl Harbor and their murder of our prisoners of war. The only language they seem to understand is the one we have been using to bombard them.

When you have to deal with a beast you have to treat him as a beast. It is most regrettable but nevertheless true.

Sincerely yours,

HARRY S. TRUMAN

Mr. Samuel McCrea Cavert
General Secretary
Federal Council of
    The Churches of Christ in America
New York City, New York

CHAPTER 7

Peace

☒ *hello*

Victory brought joyful celebration in the Allied nations. The long, hard war was over, and people literally danced in the streets. As the celebrations ended, however, the victors demanded vengeance. They were angry not only that the Axis nations had started a war of aggression but also that they had conducted the war in such a brutal manner. Allied liberation of prison camps in Europe and Asia revealed horrendous mistreatment.

In Europe evidence of what the Nazis had done at death camps such as Auschwitz slowly forced the world to see what many had found unimaginable: that a nation could plan and carry out the deliberate murder of millions of Jews and others deemed subhuman. Gradually the world began to see what would become known as the Holocaust. In trials of Germans and Japanese charged as war criminals at Nuremberg and Tokyo, Allied judges began the long process of seeking justice as well as vengeance.

The bitterness and hatred of the war years would not pass quickly. To ensure that Germany and Japan would not go to war again the Allies began a military occupation, stripped them of their weapons, and attempted to force new forms of government, education, and culture on the people.

The Allies did not agree on how to treat the vanquished, however. Major divisions emerged between the Soviet Union, on the one hand, and Britain and the United States, on the other. Disagreements during the war, such as Soviet anger over delay in opening a second front, had been papered over. With peace, the differences intensified, particularly

On VE Day, May 8, 1945, Churchill waves to the enormous crowd gathered in Whitehall to celebrate the Allied victory over Germany. "In all our long history," Churchill told the cheering crowd, "we have never seen a greater day than this."

There were shouts of joy, dancing in the streets, clanging of pots and pans. . . . I was not rejoicing. The war never ended for me because my Dad never came home.

—Vicki Lacount, who was eight years old on
V-J Day, writing in a 1990 memoir

as the Soviet Union demanded control of eastern Germany, Poland, and other countries on its western border. The communist Soviet Union and capitalist United States were soon off and running in an arms race that became the Cold War.

The war left devastation, displacement, and hunger in its wake across Europe and Asia. The major exception was the United States, now the most powerful nation in the world. In America unprecedented prosperity followed the war, along with social changes that included a baby boom, questions about the proper place for women, and growing demands of equality for African Americans.

Victory

Victory brought dancing in the streets all across the Allied world. Doris J. Winiker described the raucous scene in New York City in a letter she wrote to her Army husband, Walter, on August 16, 1945.

Sailors kissed any available civilian in New York's Times Square as they celebrated the surrender of Japan in August 1945. The *New York Times* reported on August 15 that "restraint was thrown to the winds. Those in the crowds in the streets tossed hats, boxes and flags into the air. Men and women embraced—there were no strangers in New York yesterday."

Confetti and streamers were ankle deep and were being sold at every street corner and even in the middle of the gutter. Policemen and M.P.s lined each side of the gutter shoulder to shoulder, but took no heed of the goings on like the sailors and soldiers standing in the gutter and grabbing every woman and girl in their arms and passionately kissing them in spite of kicking, screaming, and protesting. People sat on the curbs of Broadway and Times square right in front of the cops and necked—but most violently! Soldiers and sailors climbed on the hoods of passing cars and police and M.P.s just stood there smiling. A sailor started after me and wouldn't give up even though I ran and ran all over the street and finally took refuge in back of a cop—but when I ask him to protect me—the cop offered to kiss me too—so unable to help myself any longer—I got kissed! (against my will—of course). Can you forgive me sugar? It was a very disturbing experience because I had forgotten what it's like to be kissed—but I didn't enjoy it—it only made me all the more lonesome for you, baby.

But even in victory celebration there were reminders of a war's costs. Dorothy Zmuda was working at her job in a Milwaukee office when news of Japan's surrender came. She later recalled her feelings in an oral history interview.

Everybody in the office said, "Everybody's going to be downtown in Milwaukee. Everybody's going to run downtown." . . . So after work we all got on the streetcars. The streetcars were just jammed with people. . . . Everybody was so happy the war was over. And the streetcar was going down National Avenue, and it came in front of Wood Hospital. . . . But here on the grounds are sitting all these veterans, some without legs, in wheelchairs with their legs covered with a blanket, and they're just sitting there watching us, watching these streetcars of mad people going past, yelling and screaming. Well, when the people spotted them everybody just quieted down and it [was] just flat [silence], and then a couple blocks later they started up again. That I remember. I could never forget that.

Victory was a time for some to reflect on the past difficulties and on their religious faith. In his diary on August 15, 1945, Britain's top military officer, Alan Brooke, did just that.

The end of this war for certain. Six very very long years of continuous struggle, nerve wracking anxiety, dashed hopes, hopeless bleak horizons, endless difficulties with Winston [Churchill], etc etc finished with! When I look back at the blackest moments it becomes almost impossible to believe that we stand where we do. One thing above all others predominates all other thoughts, namely boundless gratitude to God, and to His guiding hand which has brought us where we are. Throughout the war his guiding influence has constantly made itself felt.

In a radio address to the American people on September 1, 1945, President Harry Truman marked the Japanese surrender and the first V-J Day—victory over Japan. It was a triumphal moment.

And our thoughts go out to our gallant Allies in this war: to those who resisted the invaders; to those who were not strong enough to hold out, but who, nevertheless, kept the fires of resistance alive within the souls of their people; to those who stood up against great odds and held the line, until the United Nations together were able to supply the arms and the men with which to overcome the forces of evil.

This is a victory of more than arms alone. This is a victory of liberty over tyranny. From our war plants rolled the tanks and planes which blasted their way to the heart of our enemies; from our shipyards sprang the ships which bridged all the oceans of the world for our weapons and supplies; from our farms came the food and fiber

I have got back my weight. I lost (20 lbs.) in combat. I weigh 175 now.

—GI Ernest Eller, letter to his parents from southern Germany, May 29, 1945

Victory

Not in paradise, but on this vast tract of
   earth,
Where at every step there is sorrow, sorrow,
   sorrow,
I awaited her, as one waits only when one
   loves,
I knew her as one knows only oneself,
I knew her in blood, in mud, in grief.
The hour stuck.
The war ended.
I made my way home.
She came towards me, and we did not
   recognize each other.

—Ilya Ehrenburg, Soviet writer, May, 1945

for our armies and navies and for our Allies in all the corners of the earth; from our mines and factories came the raw materials and the finished products which gave us the equipment to overcome our enemies.

But back of it all were the will and spirit and determination of a free people—who know what freedom is, and who know that it is worth whatever price they had to pay to preserve it.

It was the spirit of liberty which gave us our armed strength and which made our men invincible in battle. We now know that that spirit of liberty, the freedom of the individual, and the personal dignity of man, are the strongest and toughest and most enduring forces in all the world.

And so on V-J Day we take renewed faith and pride in our own way of life. We have had our day of rejoicing over this victory. We have had our day of prayer and devotion. Now let us set aside V-J Day as one of renewed consecration to the principles which have made us the strongest nation on earth and which, in this war, we have striven so mightily to preserve.

The Guilty

As the war in Europe ended, the extent of Nazi brutalities became more visible. Those who saw the evidence wanted the world to know, and they wanted Germans to suffer. One was a British officer, Robert Barer, who wrote his wife on May 3, 1945, from Sandbostel, a liberated German POW camp.

Now I would believe anything—absolutely anything. The S.S. are just not human—they *must* be exterminated. It would be far better to kill a few thousand innocent ones than allow a single one of them to escape. . . . Even now I suppose people in England will not believe these things. They'll say the pictures are fake. No picture on earth could ever convey one millionth of the real horror.

Captain Barer wrote his wife again on May 8.

You may be horrified at the pictures of German women being made to bury the dead but it's the best thing that could happen. They will never forget it. I am sure there has never been anything like it in the history of the world.

As the Allies liberated concentration camps and death camps, the horrors seemed unbearable. General Dwight Eisenhower wanted others to

The Germans removed valuable wedding rings from concentration and death camp prisoners. American GIs found these rings near the Buchenwald concentration camp in May 1945.

see firsthand and sent this telegram on April 19, 1945, to General George Marshall. At this early stage there was incomplete understanding of what the Nazis had done. Eisenhower still focused on "political prisoners" rather than the millions of Jews and others murdered with no regard for their politics.

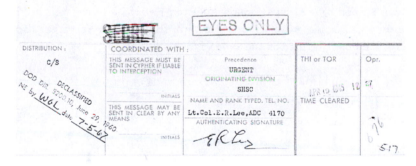

In defeat many Germans claimed they had never been Nazis. American war correspondent Martha Gellhorn bitterly mocked these claims in a story she filed from Cologne in April 1945.

No one is a Nazi. No one ever was. There may have been some Nazis in the next village. . . . Oh, the Jews? Well, there weren't really many Jews in this neighborhood. Two maybe, maybe six. They were taken away. I hid a Jew for six weeks. I hid a Jew for eight weeks. (I hid a Jew, he hid a Jew, all God's chillun hid Jews.) We have nothing against the Jews: we always got on well with them. We have waited for the Americans a long time. You came and liberated us. You came to befriend us. . . . We have done nothing wrong; we are not Nazis.

It should, we feel, be set to music. Then the Germans could sing this refrain and that would make it even better. They all talk like this. One asks oneself how the detested Nazi government, to which no one paid allegiance, managed to carry on this war for five and a half years. Obviously not a man, woman or child in Germany ever approved of the war for a minute, according to them. We stand around looking blank and contemptuous and listen to this story without friendliness and certainly without respect. To see a whole nation passing the buck is not an enlightening spectacle. . . .

It makes little or no difference to anyone around here whether the Germans are Nazis or not: they can talk their heads off; they can sing "the Star-Spangled Banner"; they are still Germans and they are not liked. None of these soldiers has forgotten yet that our dead stretch back all the way to Africa.

General Eisenhower (center) sees for himself the horror at Ohrdruf, a German concentration camp, on April 14, 1945. Five days later he sent a telegram to General George Marshall asking him to urge other leaders and journalists to come see what he had seen. Eisenhower wanted the world to know.

And there were Nazi leaders who claimed not to know. One was Joachim von Ribbentrop, Hitler's foreign minister. He was interrogated in his prison cell by American Colonel Howard Brundage on September 10, 1945. Ribbentrop died on the gallows for his crimes.

Q: Did you know that there were hundreds of thousands of people killed in concentration camps?

A: No, I certainly did not.

Q: That also is an astounding thing to me.

A: I can absolutely say 100 per cent clear, that I did not. . . .

Q: I grant you it is secret but you cannot have hundreds of thousands of people dying in concentration camps and not know.

A: Is that true, Colonel?

Q: I think it is conservative. I think millions is nearer.

A: I can't imagine that.

Q: There are lots of things you can't imagine. You have an education coming to you.

Some Germans really did not know what their government was doing. One was Elfie Walther, a German schoolgirl whom the British forced to work in a liberated concentration camp. Shocked by what she saw, she wrote the following in her diary on May 2, 1945.

Nobody at home would believe us if we told them about it. I couldn't stop thinking about how we had loved and honoured the *Fuhrer*. Everything that he told us was a lie! What is this thing that was called National Socialism? We always thought that it was something beautiful and noble.

Why is everything so cruel? Why do they kill innocent, helpless people? One can't treat one's enemies like that! It is incomprehensible. Last night I finished with everything that I used to believe was good. People are vile pigs—all of them, all of them, including me. And there is meant to be a God? And he allows all this to happen? . . . How can we apologize?

What should be done about crimes committed at Dachau, Auschwitz, and the other camps? At the war crimes trials in the German city of Nuremberg in 1945–1946 Allied judges heard leading Nazis swear that they were only following orders and did not know about the mistreatment of prisoners and the murder of so many millions. Nineteen defendants were judged guilty; twelve of these were sentenced to death. Trials of other Nazis followed.

Among the most powerful witnesses at the Nuremberg trials was a thirty-three-year-old French woman interned at Auschwitz. On January 28, 1946, Charles Dubost, a French prosecutor, called as witness Marie Claude Vaillant-Couturier. The transcript records her description of what happened when the trains with Jews arrived at the death camp.

M. Dubost: Were you an eye witness of the selections on the arrival
of the convoys?

Mme. Vaillant-Couturier: Yes, because when we worked at the sewing block in 1944, the block where we lived directly faced the stopping place of the trains. The system had been improved. Instead of making the selection at the place where they arrived,

American troops watch a cart filled with corpses being removed from the Dachau concentration camp for burial; local farmers were required to drive the carts through town to educate the inhabitants. Bernard Rice, a combat medic who visited Dachau, remembered, "Even our bloodiest battle could not prepare us for Dachau. There we found hundreds of dead. Some lay in grotesque piles, some neatly stacked like cordwood, others thrown helter-skelter into a pit."

SS Lt. Heinz Tomhardt was among forty-three German soldiers sentenced to death by the American Military Tribunal on July 16, 1946, for his part in the massacre of American prisoners of war at Malmedy, Belgium. His sentence was later reduced to a prison term.

a side line now took the train practically right up to the gas chamber; and the stopping place, about 100 meters from the gas chamber, was right opposite our block though, of course, separated from us by two rows of barbed wire. Consequently, we saw the unsealing of the cars and the soldiers letting men, women, and children out of them. We then witnessed heart-rending scenes; old couples forced to part from each other, mothers made to abandon their young daughters, since the latter were sent to the camp, whereas mothers and children were sent to the gas chambers. All these people were unaware of the fate awaiting them. They were merely upset at being separated, but they did not know that they were going to their death. To render their welcome more pleasant at this time—June–July 1944—an orchestra composed of internees, all young and pretty girls dressed in little white blouses and navy blue skirts, played during the selection, at the arrival of the trains, gay tunes such as "The Merry Widow," the "Barcarolle" from "The Tales of Hoffman," and so forth. They were then informed that this was a labor camp and since they were not brought into the camp they saw only the small platform surrounded by flowering plants. Naturally, they could not realize what was in store for them. Those selected for the gas chamber, that is, the old people, mothers, and children, were escorted to a red-brick building.

M. Dubost: These were not given an identification number?

Mme. Vaillant-Couturier: No.

M. Dubost: They were not tattooed?

Mme. Vaillant-Couturier: No. They were not even counted.

M. Dubost: You were tattooed?

Mme. Vaillant-Couturier: Yes, look. [The witness showed her arm.] They were taken to a red brick building, which bore the letters "Baden," that is to say "Baths." There, to begin with, they were made to undress and given a towel before they went into the so-called shower room. Later on, at the time of the large convoys from Hungary, they had no more time left to play-act or to pretend; they were brutally undressed, and I know these details as I knew a little Jewess from France who lived with her family at the "Republique" district.

M. Dubost: In Paris?

Mme. Vaillant-Couturier: In Paris. She was called "little Marie" and she was the only one, the sole survivor of a family of nine. Her mother and her seven brothers and sisters had been gassed on arrival. When I met her she was employed to undress the babies before they were taken into the gas chamber. Once the people were undressed they took them into a room which was somewhat like a shower room, and gas capsules were thrown through an opening in the ceiling. An SS man would watch the effect produced through a porthole. At the end of 5 or 7 minutes, when the gas had completed its work, he gave the signal to open the doors; and men with gas masks—they too were internees—went into the room and removed the corpses. They told us that the internees must have suffered before dying, because they were closely clinging to one another and it was very difficult to separate them.

After that a special squad would come to pull out gold teeth and dentures; and again, when the bodies had been reduced to ashes, they would sift them in an attempt to recover the gold.

At Auschwitz there were eight crematories but, as from 1944, these proved insufficient. The SS had large pits dug by the internees, where they put branches, sprinkled with gasoline, which they set on fire. Then they threw the corpses into the pits. From our block we could see after about three-quarters of an hour or an hour after the arrival of a convoy, large flames coming from the crematory, and the sky was lighted up by the burning pits.

The Allies also charged Japanese leaders with waging an aggressive war and committing war crimes and crimes against humanity. At the Tokyo war crimes trials, beginning in May 1946, the Allies focused on Japanese treatment of prisoners and the brutalities the army committed in China, especially those that were known as the Rape of Nanking. Seven of those found guilty were hanged, including Tojo. Also executed was the top Japanese officer in China, General Matsui Iwane, who was found guilty of failing to stop war crimes committed under his command in Nanking in 1937. The court handed down this verdict against Matsui on November 12, 1948.

In this period of six or seven weeks thousands of women were raped, upwards of 100,000 people were killed and untold property was stolen and burned. At the height of these dreadful happenings, on 17 December, MATSUI made a triumphal entry into the City and remained there from five to seven days. From his own observations and from the reports of his staff he must have been aware of what was happening. He admits he was told of some degree of misbehavior of his Army. . . . Daily reports of these atrocities were made to

One of the Tokyo Trial Judges, Radhabinod Pal of India, voted against the majority and found General Matsui innocent.

The steps thus taken by General MATSUI proved ineffective. But there is no suggestion that these were in any way insincere. On this evidence, I cannot ascribe any deliberate and reckless disregard of legal duty on the part of General Matsui in this respect.

Judge Pal was among those who asserted that the Tokyo and Nuremberg trials were "victors' justice." Hatreds created by the war drove convictions, he believed, not real justice.

It has been said that a victor can dispense to the vanquished everything from mercy to vindictiveness; but the one thing the victor cannot give to the vanquished is justice.

Tokyo Trial Judge B. V. A. Röling, from the Netherlands, recalled that some young Japanese accused the court of a double standard.

Are you morally entitled to sit in judgment over the leaders of Japan when the Allies have burned down all of its cities with sometimes, as in Tokyo, in one night, 100,000 deaths and which culminated in the destruction of Hiroshima and Nagasaki? Those were war crimes.

Newly liberated British POWS relax in Singapore in August 1945. Like many Allied prisoners of the Japanese, they had suffered severe malnutrition.

Japanese diplomatic representative in Nanking who, in turn, reported them to Tokyo. The Tribunal is satisfied that MATSUI knew what was happening. He did nothing, or nothing effective to abate these horrors. He did issue orders before the capture of the City enjoining propriety of conduct upon his troops and later he issued further orders to the same purport. These orders were of no effect as is now known, and as he must have known. It was pleaded on his behalf that at the time he was ill. His illness was not sufficient to prevent his conducting the military operations of his command nor to prevent his visiting the City for days while these atrocities were occurring. He was in command of the Army responsible for these happenings. He knew of them. He had the power, as he had the duty, to control his troops and to protect the unfortunate citizens of Nanking. He must be held criminally responsible for his failure to discharge his duty....

Accused, MATSUI, Iwane, on the Counts of the Indictment on which you have been convicted, the International Military Tribunal for the Far East sentences you to death by hanging.

Occupation

To ensure peace Allied troops began a hard occupation of the defeated countries. The United States government showed GIs a film made in 1945 titled *Your Job in Germany*. Theodore Geisel (later known as Dr. Seuss) wrote this text for the film's narration.

The problem now is future peace. That is your job in Germany. By your conduct and attitude while on guard inside Germany, you can lay the groundwork of a peace that could last forever, or just the opposite. You could lay the groundwork for a new war to come. And, just as American soldiers had to do this job 26 years ago, so other American soldiers, your sons, might have to do it again another 20-odd years from now. Germany today appears to be beaten. Hitler out. Swastikas gone. Nazi propaganda off the air. Concentration camps empty. You'll see ruins. You'll see flowers. You'll see some mighty pretty scenery. Don't let it fool you. You are in enemy country. Be alert. Suspicious of everyone. Take no chances. You are up against something more than tourist scenery. You are up against German history. It isn't good...

You will not be friendly. You will be aloof, watchful and suspicious. Every German is a potential source of trouble. Therefore, there must be no fraternization with any of the German people. Fraternization means making friends. The German people are not our friends. You will not associate with German men, women or children. You will not associate with them on familiar terms either in public or in private. You will not visit in their homes nor will you ever take them into your confidence. However friendly, however sorry, however sick of the Nazi party they may seem, they cannot come back into the civilized fold just by sticking out their hand and saying, "I'm sorry." Don't clasp that hand. It's not the kind of hand you can clasp in friendship. . . . Trust none of them. Someday the German people might be cured of their disease. The super race disease. The world conquest disease. But they must prove that they have been cured beyond the shadow of a doubt before they ever again are allowed to take their place among respectable nations. Until that day we stand guard.

The occupation of Germany was complicated by divided control among the United States, France, Great Britain, and the Soviet Union, as proposed at the Yalta Conference and elsewhere. The U.S. military occupiers stated their goals in this directive issued on May 10, 1945, which attempted not only to punish Germans but also to build a lasting democracy. The directive included orders for German schools.

The principal Allied objective is to prevent Germany from ever again becoming a threat to the peace of the world. Essential steps in the accomplishment of this objective are the elimination of Nazism and militarism in all their forms, the immediate apprehension of war criminals for punishment, the industrial disarmament and demilitarization of Germany, with continuing control over Germany's capacity to make war, and the preparation for an eventual reconstruction of German political life on a democratic basis. . . .

A coordinated system of control over German education and an affirmative program of reorientation will be established designed completely to eliminate Nazi and militaristic doctrines and to encourage the development of democratic ideas. . . . Textbooks and

The Americans allowed Japan's Emperor Hirohito to keep his throne, even though some thought he should be tried as a war criminal. On September 27, 1945, Hirohito, in formal dress, called on American General Douglas MacArthur, who was in charge of the occupation. This famous photograph made clear to the Japanese that they had lost the war and the Americans were in charge: MacArthur is taller, more at ease, older. He made the emperor come to his office and did not bother to put on a dress uniform or medals, not even a necktie, to receive an emperor who had once claimed to be divine.

curricula which are not free of Nazi and militaristic doctrine shall not be used.

There was distrust on all sides in 1945. What would the victors do to the defeated? A Japanese sixth grader, Sasaki Naokata, had been evacuated to the countryside from Tokyo. More than four decades later, in an oral history interview, he remembered his fears when the American invaders arrived in August 1945.

The thought that Japan would lose hadn't been in our thoughts. We continued to chant "Annihilate America and England! One-Two-Three-Four!" in our morning calisthenics for two more days. Finally, our teacher told us "The war has ended." They never said, "Japan lost," just that we could go back home. That was good.

Gradually, my friends started going back to Tokyo. But not me. I couldn't yet, so there I still was, in Miyagi, on the day when word came, "The Americans are on their way! They're coming on jeeps and trucks!"

Great clouds of dust billowed up as jeeps raced down the road towards us. We peeped out through little holes we'd poked in the paper of the inn's shoji screens to try to catch a glimpse of them. What would they be like? Suddenly, it occurred to us, "They must have horns!" We had images of glaring demons with horns spouting from their heads.

We were disappointed, of course. No horns at all. Later, school-mates who'd bumped into them on the streets brought back choco-lates. "Americans, they're good people," they said, but I told them that couldn't be true. I swore that they must be lying. But I never went out to see for myself, not until I got back to Tokyo, anyway.

The American occupation of Japan lasted from 1945 until 1952. The victors imposed strict limits on Japanese freedoms while they attempted to eliminate Japanese militarism and create an American-style democracy. Article 9 of the new Japanese constitution, written by the Americans, renounced war.

Aspiring sincerely to an international peace based on justice and order, the Japanese people forever renounce war as a sovereign right of the nation and the threat or use of force as means of settling international disputes.

In order to accomplish the aim of the preceding paragraph, land, sea, and air forces, as well as other war potential, will never be maintained. The right of belligerency of the state will not be recognized.

Small green vegetables
are growing in the rain
along the burned street

—Japanese poem describing the gardens peopled planted next to bombed ruins, and censored by the Americans as too critical of the United States

The only woman among the Japanese Constitution's American drafters was Beate Sirota. Born to a Jewish family in Vienna, she grew up in Japan, went to college in California, and then worked for the U.S. government and *Time* magazine during the war. Fluent in Japanese, Sirota had primary responsibility for articles regarding equal rights. The new Constitution she helped write was among the most liberal in the world, although traditions of inequality would endure.

Article 14. All of the people are equal under the law and there shall be no discrimination in political, economic or social relations because of race, creed, sex, social status or family origin. . . .

Article 24. Marriage shall be based only on the mutual consent of both sexes and it shall be maintained through mutual cooperation with the equal rights of husband and wife as a basis.

(2) With regard to choice of spouse, property rights, inheritance, choice of domicile, divorce and other matters pertaining to marriage and the family, laws shall be enacted from the standpoint of individual dignity and the essential equality of the sexes.

In her memoir, published in 1997 and titled No Woman in the Room, *Beate Sirota recalled working on the Japanese Constitution.*

I tried to imagine the kinds of changes that would most benefit Japanese women, who had almost always married men chosen for them by their parents, walked behind their husbands, and carried their babies on their backs. Husbands divorced wives just because they could not have children. Women had no property rights. It was clear that their rights in general would have to be set forth explicitly.

From Hunger to a Better World?

The end of war was not the end of suffering for the many who became displaced persons—DPs for short. An American Red Cross worker from Alabama, Harriett Engelhardt, wrote to her parents on April 21, 1945, describing what she saw as she entered Germany.

Those who make such estimates say there are at least 17 million displaced persons—we saw at least 15 million of them—walking, walking, walking down that super Auto-bahn, four lanes of traffic through the immense and beautiful and grand plains of Germany, with no food, water, shelter or clothing. Pushing or pulling a little cart with perhaps a couple of blankets on it, or a small dog. Men and women—Czechs, Poles, Russians, French, Belgian, Dutch—slave laborers, captured soldiers, or freed political prisoners. Tired to exhaustion, starved, and cold—but free. Thousands will die of exhaustion and exposure. . . . The flags of many nations fly over bicycle and baby carriages and little wagons, and many languages babble from tired faces. . . . It is very strange

The American bombing of Japanese cities left many families homeless, including this one in Tokyo. One American observed that "the streets of every major city quickly became peopled with demoralized ex-soldiers, war widows, orphans, the homeless and unemployed—most of them preoccupied with simply staving off hunger."

Americans contributed many millions of dollars in food and economic aid in Europe and Asia after 1945. But not all Americans approved. A resident of Lincoln, Nebraska, Dorothy Westcott, wrote President Truman on May 15, 1946.

Why don't you stop worrying about the children of Europe and Asia and start considering the children, if not the adults, of the United States of America? . . . Feeding the Germans and the Japs is just feeding another war: they will have no respect for us if we feed them—only contempt. Make the Germans and the Japs suffer the consequences of their own folly and fiendishness.

to see a German farmer plodding doggedly over his field behind a plow, with a white flag fluttering from his horse's collar.

And hunger remained. President Truman appointed former President Herbert Hoover to assess the situation. In a radio broadcast heard by millions on May 17, 1946, Hoover described what he had learned on his recent trip around the world.

Along the 35,000 miles we have traveled, I have seen with my own eyes the grimmest specter of famine in all the history of the world.

Of the Four Horsemen of the Apocalypse, the one named War has gone—at least for a while. But Famine, Pestilence and Death are still charging over the earth. . . . Never have so many evil Horsemen come all at one time.

Hunger hangs over the homes of more than 800,000,000 people—over one-third of the people of the earth. Hunger is a silent visitor who comes like a shadow. He sits beside every anxious mother three times each day. He brings not alone suffering and sorrow, but fear and terror. He carries disorder and the paralysis of government, and even its downfall. He is more destructive than armies, not only in human life but in morals. All of the values of right living melt before his invasions, and every gain of civilization crumbles. But we can save these people from the worst, if we will.

For most Americans peace brought far more opportunities than had existed during the Great Depression of the 1930s, partly because of the GI Bill of Rights. When he signed the bill on June 22, 1944, President Roosevelt pointed to several benefits, including financial aid that enabled a massive number of veterans to go to college and low-cost mortgages that enabled them to buy houses. Roosevelt could not see clearly the period of great economic prosperity that would follow the war for many Americans.

This bill, which I have signed today, substantially carries out most of the recommendations made by me. . . .

1. It gives servicemen and women the opportunity of resuming their education or technical training after discharge, or of taking a refresher or retrainer course, not only without tuition charge up to $500 per school year, but with the right to receive a monthly living allowance while pursuing their studies.
2. It makes provision for the guarantee by the Federal Government of not to exceed 50 percent of certain loans made

to veterans for the purchase or construction of homes, farms, and business properties.

3. It provides for reasonable unemployment allowances payable each week up to a maximum period of one year, to those veterans who are unable to find a job.

4. It establishes improved machinery for effective job counseling for veterans and for finding jobs for returning soldiers and sailors.

5. It authorizes the construction of all necessary additional hospital facilities.

6. It strengthens the authority of the Veterans Administration to enable it to discharge its existing and added responsibilities with promptness and efficiency.

With the signing of this bill a well-rounded program of special veterans' benefits is nearly completed. It gives emphatic notice to the men and women in our armed forces that the American people do not intend to let them down.

In addition to economic growth in the United States the war produced growth in family size. Writing in *Ladies' Home Journal* on September 19, 1944, Amram Scheinfeld provided an early comment on what would be called the "baby boom" and a suggestion that women would be happier in the kitchen and nursery than in jobs and careers. Images of Rosie the Riveter would soon fade—only to reemerge during the women's rights movement of the 1970s.

When young Mrs. Betty Conrad, of Minneapolis, comes out enthusiastically for big families—and proves it by having seven children, with ten as her goal—she may not realize it, but she's the harbinger of a new American trend. Our population experts and other authorities foresee a growing popularity for large families, not only because a war-ravaged world will want more children, but because increasing numbers of women, disillusioned with their present roles or with what the workaday world can offer, will turn toward motherhood as the happiest road to fulfillment.

Contributing enormously to this trend will be these wartime influences: Vast numbers of young American women have embarked on childbearing much earlier than usual, and have found motherhood to their liking; millions of women in war jobs are now convinced they'll be happier as homemakers when their duty is done; and returning servicemen will be hungry for family life. . . .

Peace and returning soldiers brought to America a shortage of housing and an abundance of babies, as suggested by this photograph of a veterans' trailer park in Charlottesville, Virginia.

A huge proportion of women engaged in war work have indicated, through various surveys, that they will have had their fill of jobs when the emergency is over and, with a new appreciation of the home sphere, will welcome the role of mother. Then there will be the tremendous psychological impact of the returning servicemen. The overwhelming majority of G.I. Joes have this thought uppermost: to settle down when it's over with a "womanly" wife, and to have a houseful of kids.

Not all women agreed with Amram Scheinfeld's assessment. One was a skilled worker on Long Island, New York, who, like many others, lost her wartime job because she was a woman. Ottilie Juliet Gattuso stated her case in a letter to President Truman.

September 6, 1945

President Truman

Dear President,

This letter is in reference to the unemployment situation on Long Island, New York. Now that the war is won and over, there are no jobs with a living wage available.

I was one of the first women to be employed by the Grumman Aircraft Engineering Corp. back in March of 1942, now I am given to understand that the Grumman Corp. will not rehire any women *in their shop.*

The only jobs open to women are office jobs which pay an average wage of $20.00 to $22.00 a week. I happen to be a widow with a mother and son to support and no other means of income. I pay $45.00 a month for rent exclusive of my gas and light and at the present time there is no cheaper place to rent on Long Island. Those being the conditions, I am unable to manage on a $22.00 a week salary.

My reason for writing to you is not for pity, but I would like to know why, after serving a company in good faith for almost 3 1/2 years, is it now impossible to obtain employment with them. I am a lathe hand and was classified as skilled labor, but simply because I happen to be a woman I am not wanted.

Won't you kindly look into these matters and see that the women who are considered the head of a family get as much of an even break as the men.

Sincerely yours,

Ottilie Juliet Gattuso
30 Shepherd Ave.,
Lynbrook, New York

Wartime disruption of family life included an increase in children born to unmarried parents. A U.S. government pamphlet published in 1945, titled *Services for Unmarried Mothers and Their Children*, alerted social service personnel to family challenges that would continue after the war.

The problem of the unmarried mother and her child is an old one that was increased and accentuated by the war. Conditions created by the needs for rapidly expanded industry placed great strain upon families and individuals. People moved in large numbers to war-industry areas and to areas adjacent to Army camps and Naval stations. Although the individual's needs were the same in the new as in the old community they were less easily met. Old community ties were broken abruptly; new ones were not formed quickly. . . .

The entry of large numbers of men into the armed forces had a disrupting effect upon the relationships of men and women. Young people in all walks of life who under normal conditions would be looking forward to courtship, marriage, and establishment of their own homes and families felt insecure about the present and future. Some developed a live-for-today philosophy that lost sight of long-time values. Adolescent girls, especially, were sometimes misled by their eagerness to do something for the youths going away to hardship and danger. Husbands and wives, in many instances married too short a time to have established a firm foundation for their married life, suffered from the anxieties and loneliness of separation.

Many of these situations will not change immediately with the close of the war; some of them, or similar situations, will persist through a considerable proportion of the reconversion period. Both families and individuals will face serious problems in the readjustment to peacetime ways of living. . . .

Many months will pass before demobilization is completed and perhaps several years before some young men and women feel sufficiently secure to marry and establish their own homes.

Such conditions explain in part the number of illegitimate births that occur yearly.

During the war Walter White, head of the National Association for the Advancement of Colored People (NAACP), traveled to Europe and Africa to assess conditions facing African-American soldiers. He published his findings in 1945 in a book titled *A Rising Wind*, in which he connected white racial discrimination at home with discrimination and imperialism around the world. White's assessment anticipated the American

civil rights movement and the movements in Asia and Africa for independence from colonial powers.

World War II has immeasurably magnified the Negro's awareness of the disparity between the American profession and practice of democracy....

When there is added to that the vigorous efforts of many white Americans to spread the poison of race hatred in their countries, even as the war against Hitler was being fought, one has no difficulty in understanding why the Negro veteran will return to America disillusioned and cynical. America has no one else but herself to blame for such a state of mind. Yet the Negro soldier's attitude is not one of defeatist disillusionment. The majority of Negro soldiers will return home convinced that whatever betterment of their lot is achieved must come largely through their own efforts. They will return determined to use those efforts to the utmost.

World War II has given to the Negro a sense of kinship with other colored—and also—oppressed peoples of the world. Where he has not thought through or informed himself on the racial angles of colonial policy and master-race theories, he senses that the struggle of the Negro in the United States is part and parcel of the struggle against imperialism and exploitation in India, China, Burma, Africa, the Philippines, Malay, the West Indies, and south America. The Negro soldier is convinced that as time proceeds that the identification of interests will spread even among some brown and yellow peoples who today refuse to see the connection between their exploitation by white nations and discrimination against the Negro in the United States....

A wind *is* rising—a wind of determination by the have-nots of the world to share the benefits of freedom and prosperity which the haves of the earth have tried to keep exclusively for themselves. That wind blows all over the world. Whether that wind develops into a hurricane is a decision which we must make now and in the days when we form the peace.

Black workers increasingly claimed full rights of citizenship after the war, including recognition as labor union members. Here, members of the United Packinghouse Workers of America strike in Montgomery, Alabama, in 1951.

With the suffering of war fresh in their minds, the victorious nations formed the United Nations in 1945. In seeking to keep the peace the new international organization adopted on December 10, 1948, its Universal Declaration of Human Rights. The preamble to the document explained why all people deserved fundamental rights, whatever their nationality, race, or sex.

Whereas recognition of the inherent dignity and of the equal and inalienable rights of all members of the human family is the foundation of freedom, justice and peace in the world,

Whereas disregard and contempt for human rights have resulted in barbarous acts which have outraged the conscience of mankind, and the advent of a world in which human beings shall enjoy freedom of speech and belief and freedom from fear and want has been proclaimed as the highest aspiration of the common people,

Whereas it is essential, if man is not to be compelled to have recourse, as a last resort, to rebellion against tyranny and oppression, that human rights should be protected by the rule of law,

Whereas it is essential to promote the development of friendly relations between nations,

Whereas the peoples of the United Nations have in the Charter reaffirmed their faith in fundamental human rights, in the dignity and worth of the human person and in the equal rights of men and women and have determined to promote social progress and better standards of life in larger freedom,

Whereas Member States have pledged themselves to achieve, in co-operation with the United Nations, the promotion of universal respect for and observance of human rights and fundamental freedoms,

Whereas a common understanding of these rights and freedoms is of the greatest importance for the full realization of this pledge.

Now, Therefore THE GENERAL ASSEMBLY proclaims THIS UNIVERSAL DECLARATION OF HUMAN RIGHTS as a common standard of achievement for all peoples and all nations, to the end that every individual and every organ of society, keeping this Declaration constantly in mind, shall strive by teaching and education to promote respect for these rights and freedoms and by progressive measures, national and international, to secure their universal and effective recognition and observance, both among the peoples of Member States themselves and among the peoples of territories under their jurisdiction.

War Memories

Situated above the D-Day landing beach, the American Cemetery at Normandy contains 9,387 graves, each with a perfectly aligned Latin cross or Star of David of white marble set into the grass. The site evokes a sense of order and peace, softening the horror of war. Few American visitors leave without shedding tears.

At its end, many wanted to forget World War II. Survivors sought home and comfort and a new life in peace and prosperity. It was easier for Americans to forget than for most other people, especially those citizens in the defeated nations who lived under the victors' occupation.

Forgetting was impossible, but what people remembered varied greatly. In America some would eventually label this a "good war." Some have even claimed that this was America's "greatest generation ever." But there were memories also of a not-so-good war, even a bad war. Around the world individuals pondered the physical and emotional turmoil of combat, prison camps, bombs, and hunger. Most troubling was the Holocaust, which over time grew in its horror and pulled thoughtful citizens to contemplate the human condition.

As time passed many who experienced World War II began to talk more about it. Some wanted to celebrate and commemorate. Those with grievances grew more outspoken and began to demand apology and redress. Few agreed on what had happened and what it meant. In memorials and museums and in popular culture as well as in history books, many insisted that this war never be forgotten. And for most, there remained a conviction that Allied victory over the Axis powers was an absolute necessity.

Many combat veterans remained silent especially about things that contradicted "good war" notions. Three decades after the war Jack Short told an interviewer:

I never discuss what I did in the service with my children. I told them some of the funnier stories. They do not know all the things that happened during the World War. I prefer that they don't.

America's "good war" myth required believing that GIs were all good in all ways, including traditional sexual morals. Writer John Steinbeck in his book Once There Was a War, *published in 1958, mocked the assumption:*

That five million perfectly normal, young energetic and concupiscent men and boys had for the period of the War Effort put aside their habitual preoccupation with girls. The fact that they carried pictures of nude girls, called pin-ups, did not occur to anyone as paradox. The convention was the law. When Army supply ordered X millions of rubber contraceptive and disease-preventing items, it had to be explained that they were used to keep moisture out of machine-gun barrels—and perhaps they did.

The "Good War" and Other Memories

Many Americans tried to remember the most positive aspects of the war. On August 15, 1945, Marjorie Haselton wrote her husband, Richard, who had been fighting in China. She presented an early version of what would become "the greatest generation ever" argument.

You and I were brought up to think cynically of patriotism—not by our parents, but by the books, plays, movies and magazine features written by the bitter, realistic writers of the twenties and thirties. They called patriotism a tool of the demagogues, a spell binder to blind our eyes to the "real" truth. We thought they were right—at least, I know, I did. I hated everything in music, books, movies, etc. that stressed love of country. That was for the yokels. The uninitiated, but not for anyone who really was in the know. Maybe I was right—I don't know. One thing I AM sure of—a thing this war has taught me—I love my country and I'm not ashamed to admit it anymore. Perhaps I am only thinking along the lines the nation's propagandists want me to think. But I know I am proud of the men of my generation. Brought up like you and I, in false prosperity then degrading depression, they have overcome these handicaps. And shown the world that America has something the world can never take away from us—a determination to keep our way of life.

Underneath what the Jap[anese] and the Germans believe to be a "what-the-hell," decadent attitude—you boys proved that you had a fighting spirit and team work that couldn't be beaten. Call it Yankee ingenuity or whatever you will, it still is the one force that won the war—the thing the enemy never believed we had. That is why, tonight, I am proud to be an American, and married to one of its fighting men. None of you fellows wanted the deal life handed you—but just about every one of you gritted your teeth and hung on. "Do the job, get it over with, and get home again" was the byword. You proved that Americans may look soft and easy going, "spoiled" by the highest standard of living in the world, yet when the hour of need came you showed them we could take it—*and* dish it out.

Some veterans came home with physical wounds, some with emotional scars. Chicagoan Peggy Terry remembered one kind of war casualty in this interview decades later with oral historian Studs Terkel.

My husband was a paratrooper in the war, in the 101st Airborne Division. He made twenty-six drops in France, North Africa, and Germany. I look back at the war with sadness. I wasn't smart enough to think too deeply then. We had a lotta good times and we had money and we had food on the table and the rent was paid. Which had never happened to us before. But when I look back and think of him . . .

Until the war he never drank. He never even smoked. When he came back he was an absolute drunkard. And he used to have the most awful nightmares. He'd get up in the middle of the night and start screaming. I'd just sit for hours and hold him while he just shook. We'd go to the movies, and if they'd have films with a lot of shooting in it, he'd just start to shake and have to get up and leave. He started slapping me around and slapped the kids around. He became a brute.

My Pacific war experiences have haunted me, and it has been a burden to retain this story. But time heals, and the nightmares no longer wake me in a cold sweat with pounding heart and racing pulse.

—Marine veteran Eugene Sledge, in his memoir published in 1981

War correspondent Vasily Grossman, even more than many of his fellow Soviet citizens, suffered under the Stalinist dictatorship of the postwar years. But Grossman never lost faith in the righteousness of the "Great Patriotic War" and of the Soviet men and women who fought it. Grossman's daughter, Ekaterina, recalled in her memoir a song her father first heard at the Battle of Stalingrad.

A large empty room. Twilight—because evening is coming, or perhaps rain. There are three of us in the room, Papa, my stepbrother Fedya and I. . . . We are singing some songs from the war. Father would start in a stern, thundering voice. His unmusical ear did not prove too great a problem. The simple melody was so familiar to us:

A gigantic statue of Mother Russia, sword upraised, commemorates the victory at Stalingrad in 1943. On the sixtieth anniversary of the battle, in 2003, veterans, officials, and ordinary citizens gathered there to remember the "great patriotic war."

> The aircraft is spinning around,
> It is roaring, it's flying down towards the Earth's breast. . . .

But now my father stands up. Fedya and I stand up too. Father is standing there stooping, his hands at his side as if he were on parade. His face is solemn and stern.

> Arise, the huge country.
> Arise for the mortal battle.
> With the dark fascist force,
> With the accursed horde.

My father considered this song a work of genius: he said so often and with much conviction. . . He always stood up when he sang it.

Private memories from childhood carried heavy weight. The son of a Canadian soldier wrote decades later about the father who died in Italy when he was three years old.

I can't remember how I felt when told of his death, not knowing the meaning of the word. But as I grew in consciousness, his absence became a fact of my life—like being a boy and not a girl, or living with people who were my family and not somebody else's. I came to realize I would never see him, but it wasn't something I could rationally get my mind around.

Because everybody else I knew had a father, I felt set apart, like one of the strange people hidden in backrooms or attics. It also meant I didn't have an obvious and recognizable identity: I didn't belong to Dr. X or Shift Boss Y. However, I did have a privileged spiritual link. While my classmates uttered abstractions during the daily rote muttering of the Lord's Prayer, I had a picture in my mind of "Our Father, who art in Heaven."

The memoir *Night,* published in 1958, made Elie Wiesel one of the best-known Holocaust survivors. In 1986 Wiesel received the Nobel Peace Prize. This photograph of prisoners in their sleeping bunks at Buchenwald in 1945 shows Wiesel in the second row, seventh from the left, next to the vertical support beam.

Atrocities and Apologies

Struggles over the meaning of the Holocaust grew gradually to dominate many memories of the war. Holocaust survivors would never forget, as Elie Wiesel wrote so movingly in his book *Night*, first published in English in 1958.

Never shall I forget that night, the first night in camp, which has turned my life into one long night, seven times cursed and seven times sealed. Never shall I forget that smoke. Never shall I forget the little faces of the children, whose bodies I saw turned into wreaths of smoke beneath a silent blue sky.

Never shall I forget those flames which consumed my faith forever.

Never shall I forget that nocturnal silence which deprived me, for all eternity, of the desire to live. Never shall I forget those moments which murdered my God and my soul and turned my dreams to dust. Never shall I forget these things, even if am condemned to live as long as God Himself. Never.

Children learned about the Nazi murder of Jews from photographs in magazines or movie newsreels. One such child was Maurice Sendak, who as author of *Where the Wild Things Are* and other stories became one of America's most popular children's authors. In an interview in the *New York Times* in 1988 Sendak recalled his childhood fears.

The war I grew up with was World War II, and you think about what happened to children then, what happened to children who were my age; what happened to them, and not to me, because they lived over there, and I lived over here. When I had my bar mitzvah, they were dead. And yet they should have had their bar mitzvahs just like me. And why was I having one, and why were they not? And the photographs of children with their solemn faces and their big ears sticking out. Who were they?

Among the atrocities in Asia that did not became public knowledge until the 1980s was the Japanese military's forced sexual slavery of conquered women. Fifteen-year-old Maria Rosa Henson was fighting with Filipina guerillas in the spring of 1943 when she was captured and taken to a Japanese military garrison. Fifty years later she wrote her memoir of nine months as a "comfort woman."

Japan forced many women from all over Asia into brothels to serve Japanese military men. One of many thousands of so-called comfort women, this recently liberated Chinese girl tells her story to an Allied officer in Burma.

The following day was hell. Without warning, a Japanese soldier entered my room and pointed his bayonet at my chest. I thought he was going to kill me, but he used his bayonet to slash my dress and tear it open. I was too frightened to scream. And then he raped me. When he was done, other soldiers came into my room, and they took turns raping me.

Twelve soldiers raped me in quick succession. After which I was given half an hour to rest. Then twelve more soldiers followed. They all lined up outside the room waiting for their turn. . . .

Every day, anywhere from ten to over twenty soldiers raped me. There were times when there were as many as thirty: they came to the garrison in truckloads. At other times there were only a few soldiers, and we finished early.

Although different from the grievances of former comfort women or Holocaust survivors, the Japanese Americans interned by the United States government began in the early 1970s to seek apology and redress. A turning point came on February 19, 1976, when, in celebration of the nation's bicentennial, President Gerald R. Ford offered this proclamation. His statement helped open the door for the Civil Rights Act of 1988, which included an official apology and a reparations payment of $20,000 to each then-living survivor of internment.

In this Bicentennial Year, we are commemorating the anniversary dates of many great events in American history. An honest reckoning, however, must include a recognition of our national mistakes as well as our national achievements. Learning from our mistakes is not pleasant, but as a great philosopher once admonished, we must do so if we want to avoid repeating them.

February 19th is the anniversary of a sad day in American history. It was on that date in 1942, in the midst of the response to the hostilities that began on December 7, 1941, that Executive Order 9066 was issued, subsequently enforced by the criminal penalties of a statute enacted March 21, 1942, resulting in the uprooting of loyal Americans. Over one hundred thousand persons of Japanese ancestry were removed from their homes, detained in special camps, and eventually relocated.

The tremendous effort by the War Relocation Authority and concerned Americans for the welfare of these Japanese-Americans may add perspective to that story, but it does not erase the setback to fundamental American principles. Fortunately, the Japanese-American community in Hawaii was spared the indignities suffered by those on our mainland.

With help from a member of the Japanese American Citizens League, a former internee applies for reparations provided by Congress in 1988.

We now know what we should have known then—not only was that evacuation wrong, but Japanese-Americans were and are loyal Americans. On the battlefield and at home, Japanese-Americans—names like Hamada, Mitsumori, Marimoto, Noguchi, Yamasaki, Kido, Munemori and Miyamura—have been and continue to be written in our history for the sacrifices and the contributions they have made to the well-being and security of this, our common Nation.

The Executive order that was issued on February 19, 1942, was for the sole purpose of prosecuting the war with the Axis Powers, and ceased to be effective with the end of those hostilities. Because there was no formal statement of its termination, however, there is concern among many Japanese-Americans that there may yet be some life in that obsolete document. I think it appropriate, in this our Bicentennial Year, to remove all doubts on that matter, and to make clear out commitment in the future.

NOW, THEREFORE, I, GERALD R. FORD, President of the United States of America, do hereby proclaim that all authority conferred by Executive Order 9066 terminated upon the issuance of Proclamation 2714, which formally proclaimed the cessation of hostilities of World War II on December 31, 1946.

I call upon the American people to affirm with me this American Promise—that we have learned from the tragedy of that long-ago experience forever to treasure liberty and justice for each individual American, and resolve that this kind of action shall never again be repeated.

IN WITNESS THEREOF, I have hereunto set my hand this nineteenth day of February in the year of our Lord nineteen hundred seventy-six, and of the Independence of the United States of America the two hundredth.

Museums and Memorials

As time passed people felt more need to remember the war, to commemorate the sacrifices, and to honor the dead. By the early twenty-first century museums and memorials had opened all over the world. Each presented a particular interpretation of the war and sometimes caused controversy.

One of America's most bitter controversies over the memory of the war centered on plans for an exhibit about the *Enola Gay* at the

On July 30, 2007, the United States House of Representatives passed this resolution:

Resolved: That it is the sense of the House of Representatives that the Government of Japan—

(1) should formally acknowledge, apologize, and accept historical responsibility in a clear and unequivocal manner for its Imperial Armed Forces' coercion of young women into sexual slavery, known to the world as "comfort women," during its colonial and wartime occupation of Asia and the Pacific Islands from the 1930s through the duration of World War II. . . .

Paul Tibbets, pilot of the *Enola Gay,* told the press in June 1994 that the planned Smithsonian exhibit was "a damn big insult. It will leave you with the impression that you have to feel sorry for those poor Japanese because they were only defending their way of life."

Smithsonian's Air and Space Museum in Washington, D.C. As initially planned, visitors would be able to see not only the plane that dropped the atomic bomb on Hiroshima but also the devastating effects of that bomb on the city and its people. Many American veterans objected to the exhibit plan. In the April 1994 issue of *Air Force Magazine,* a veterans' publication, John T. Correll argued that veterans wanted an "objective setting" for the plane. They did not want visitors to see artifacts and photographs that suggested what happened to the people of Hiroshima.

The Smithsonian Institution acquired the *Enola Gay*—the B-29 that dropped the first atomic bomb—forty-four years ago. After a decade of deterioration in open weather, the aircraft was put into storage in 1960. Now, following a lengthy period of restoration, it will finally be displayed to the public on the fiftieth anniversary of its famous mission. The exhibition will run from May 1995 to January 1996 at the Smithsonian's National Air and Space Museum in Washington, D.C.

The aircraft will be an element in a larger exhibition called "The Cross-roads: The End of World War II, the Atomic Bomb, and the Origins of the Cold War." The context is the development of the atomic bomb and its use against the Japanese cities of Hiroshima and Nagasaki in August 1945.

The *Enola Gay*'s task was a grim one, hardly suitable for glamorization. Nevertheless, many visitors may be taken aback by what they see. That is particularly true for World War II veterans who had petitioned the museum to display the historic bomber in an objective setting.

The Smithsonian exhibition that opened in May 1995 was a victory for John Correll's view that visitors should not see what happened to the people of Hiroshima after the bomb exploded. The gleaming *Enola Gay* was the centerpiece of this commemoration of America's triumph over Japan.

The restored aircraft will be there all right, the front fifty-six feet of it, anyway. The rest of the gallery space is allotted to a program about the atomic bomb. The presentation is designed for shock effect. The exhibition plan notes that parents might find some parts unsuitable for viewing by their children.

For the "emotional center" of the exhibit, the curators are collecting burnt watches and broken wall clocks, photos of victims—which will be enlarged to life size—as well as melted and broken religious objects. One display is a schoolgirl's lunch box with remains of peas and rice reduced to carbon. To ensure that nobody misses the point, "where possible, photos of the persons who owned or wore these artifacts would be used to show that real people stood behind the artifacts." Survivors of Hiroshima and Nagasaki will recall the horror in their own words.

The Air and Space Museum says it takes no position on the "difficult moral and political questions" involved. For the past two years, however, museum officials have been under fire from veterans groups who charge that the exhibition plan is politically biased.

Memorials became sites of commemoration and political action. West German Chancellor Willy Brandt visited Poland's capital in 1970. On January 4, 1971, *Time* magazine described a shocking moment in Brandt's visit to the Warsaw Ghetto Monument.

The Old Jewish Ghetto, Warsaw, December, 1970: His broad, ruggedly handsome face etched with lines of concern, West Germany's Chancellor Willy Brandt walks slowly to the simple granite slab that memorializes the 500,000 Jews from the city's ghetto who were massacred by the Germans during World War II. For a moment he stands with bowed head, enveloped in silence except for the soft hiss of two gas-fed candelabra. Then, as if to atone for Germany's sins against its neighbors, Brandt falls to his knees. "No people," as Willy Brandt has said, "can escape from their history."

Among the artifacts from Hiroshima withdrawn from the Smithsonian exhibition was a lunch box belonging to Watanabe Reiko, a high school student who died in the bombing. Her body was never found, only her lunch box with its charred contents. Unable to see this lunch box and similar personal items, visitors were not likely to think about the individual victims, tragic consequences, and troubling ambiguities of Hiroshima.

All of us, whether guilty or not, whether old or young must accept the past. . . . It is not a case of coming to terms with the past. That is not possible. It cannot be subsequently modified or undone. However, anyone who closes his eyes to the past is blind to the present. Whoever refuses to remember the inhumanity is prone to new risks of infection. . . . Seeking to forget makes exile all the longer; the secret of redemption lies in remembrance.

—Richard von Weizsacker, president of West Germany, on the fortieth anniversary of the end of the war

Timeline

1918
Great War (World War I) ends, with German defeat

1931
Japan invades Manchuria

1933
Adolf Hitler becomes chancellor of Germany

1935
Nazi Germany's Nuremberg Laws place restrictions on Jews

1936
American Jesse Owens wins four gold medals at the Berlin Olympics

1937
Japanese invasion of China; Rape of Nanking; Picasso paints *Guernica*; Nazis organize "Degenerate Art" exhibit

1938
Munich Pact offers appeasement to Germany

1939
Nazi-Soviet Pact; Germany invades Poland; France and Great Britain declare war on Germany

1940
Britain begins food rationing; France surrenders to Germany; Winston Churchill gives "blood, toil, tears, and sweat" speech; Germany begins bombing of Britain as preparation to invade

1941
Germany attacks the Soviet Union; Japan attacks Pearl Harbor; United States declares war on Japan; Germany and Italy declare war on United States

1942
American films *Mrs. Miniver* and *Casablanca* appear; United States interns Japanese Americans; Americans surrender to Japan in Philippines; thousands of prisoners die on Bataan Death March; America begins to ration food; Stalin issues "not a step back" order

1943
Prisoners of Japanese build Burma-Thailand Railroad; Nazis execute leaders of White Rose resistance; Soviets defeat Germans at Battle of Stalingrad; Allies defeat Germans and Italians in North Africa; Allied intensified bombing includes Hamburg; Norman Rockwell paints *Four Freedoms*; Italy surrenders to Allies

1944

D-Day, Allies invade German-held France; Nazis launch counteroffensive at Battle of the Bulge; German SS troops massacre Americans at Malmedy in Belgium; Siege of Leningrad ends; baby boom underway in United States

1945

British and American bombers destroy Dresden; Americans bomb Tokyo; Japanese defeated at Battles of Iwo Jima and Okinawa; President Roosevelt dies, Harry Truman becomes president; Hitler commits suicide; Germany surrenders; Americans drop atomic bombs on Hiroshima and Nagasaki; Soviet Union declares war on Japan; Japanese emperor announces end of war; Allied occupation of Germany and Japan begins; Nuremberg and Tokyo war crimes trials begin against leading German and Japanese figures

1947

American-written Japanese Constitution comes into effect

1958

Holocaust survivor Elie Wiesel publishes *Night*

1962

Trial of Adolf Eichmann, administrator of mass murder of Jews

1970

West German Chancellor Willy Brandt kneels at the Warsaw Ghetto Monument

1976

President Gerald Ford offers apology for internment of Japanese Americans

1993

Holocaust Memorial Museum opens in Washington, D.C.

1995

Controversy over planned *Enola Gay* exhibit in Washington, D.C.; Okinawa Cornerstone of Peace Memorial dedicated

2004

National World War II Memorial dedication in Washington, D.C., offers last big event for many aged veterans

2005

Monument to the Murdered Jews of Europe dedicated in Berlin

Further Reading

Overviews

Bess, Michael. *Choices under Fire: Moral Dimensions of World War II*. New York: Knopf, 2006.

Dear, I. C. B., and M. R. D. Foot, eds. *The Oxford Companion to World War II*. Oxford: Oxford University Press, 1995.

Keegan, John. *The Second World War*. New York: Viking, 1989.

Lyons, Michael J. *World War II: A Short History*. Upper Saddle River, N.Y.: Pearson, 2004.

Murray, Williamson, and Allan R. Millett. *A War to Be Won: Fighting the Second World War*. Cambridge: Harvard University Press, 2000.

Overy, Richard. *Why the Allies Won*. New York: W.W. Norton, 1995.

Plowright, John. *The Causes, Course and Outcomes of World War Two*. New York: Palgrave Macmillan, 2007.

Purdue, A. W. *The Second World War*. New York: St. Martin's Press, 1999.

Stolley, Richard B., ed. *Life: World War II, History's Greatest Conflict in Pictures*. Boston: Little, Brown, 2001.

Tucker, Spencer C. *The Second World War*. New York: Palgrave Macmillan, 2004.

Weinberg, Gerhard L. *A World at Arms: A Global History of World War II*. New York: Cambridge University Press, 1994.

Origins

Bell, P. M. H. *The Origins of the Second World War in Europe*. London: Longman, 2007.

Eubank, Keith. *The Road to World War II: A Documentary History*. New York: Thomas Y. Crowell, 1973.

Iriye, Akira. *Pearl Harbor and the Coming of the Pacific War: A Brief History with Documents and Essays*. Boston: Bedford, 1999.

Overy, R. J. *The Origins of the Second World War*. Second Edition. London: Longman, 1998.

Asia

Brook, Timothy, ed. *Documents on the Rape of Nanking*. Ann Arbor: University of Michigan Press, 1999.

Cook, Haruko Taya, and Theodore F. Cook, eds. *Japan at War: An Oral History*. New York: New Press, 1992.

Dower, John W. *War without Mercy: Race and Power in the Pacific War*. New York: Pantheon Books, 1986.

Hasegawa, Tsuyoshi. *Racing the Enemy: Stalin, Truman, and the Surrender of Japan*. Cambridge, Mass.: Harvard University Press, 2005.

Havens, Thomas R. H. *Valley of Darkness: The Japanese People and World War Two*. New York: W.W. Norton, 1978.

Spector, Ronald H. *Eagle against the Sun: The American War with Japan*. New York: Free Press, 1985.

Spector, Ronald H. *In the Ruins of Empire: The Japanese Surrender and the Battle for Postwar Asia*. New York: Random House, 2007.

Europe

Anonymous. *A Woman in Berlin: Eight Weeks in the Conquered City—A Diary*. New York: Metropolitan Books, 2005.

Barber, John, and Mark Harrison. *The Soviet Home Front, 1941–1945*. London: Longman, 1991.

Crew, David F. *Hitler and the Nazis: A History in Documents*. New York: Oxford University Press, 2006.

Donnelly, Mark. *Britain in the Second World War*. London: Routledge, 1999.

Keegan, John. *Winston Churchill*. New York: Penguin, 2003.

Kitchen, Martin. *The Third Reich: Charisma and Community*. London: Longman, 2008.

Lukacs, John. *Five Days in London, May 1940*. New Haven, Conn.: Yale University Press, 1999.

Merridale, Catherine. *Ivan's War: Life and Death in the Red Army, 1939–1945*. New York: Metropolitan, 2006.

Ousby, Ian. *Occupation: The Ordeal of France*. New York: St. Martin's Press, 1997.

Overy, Richard. *The Battle of Britain: The Myth and the Reality*. New York: W.W. Norton, 2000.

Overy, Richard. *Russia's War*. New York: Penguin, 1997.

Stackelberg, Roderick, and Sally A. Winkle, eds. *The Nazi Germany Sourcebook*. London: Routledge, 2002.

Taylor, Frederick. *Dresden: Tuesday 13 February 1945*. London: Bloomsbury, 2004.

Werth, Alexander. *Russia at War, 1941–1945*. New York: Carroll & Graff, 1964.

United States

Adams, Michael C. C. *The Best War Ever: America and World War II*. Baltimore: Johns Hopkins University Press, 1994.

Gluck, Sherna Berger. *Rosie the Riveter Revisited: Women, The War, and Social Change*. New York: Meridian, 1987.

Goodwin, Doris Kearns. *No Ordinary Time: Franklin and Eleanor Roosevelt: The Home Front in World War II*. New York: Simon & Shuster, 1994.

Hess, Gary R. *The United States at War, 1941–1945*. Second Edition. Wheeling, Ill.: Harlan Davidson, 2000.

Jeffries, John W. *Wartime America: The World War II Home Front*. Chicago: Ivan R. Dee, 1996.

Kennedy, David M. *The American People in World War II*. New York: Oxford University Press, 1999.

Litoff, Judy Barrett, and David C. Smith, eds. *American Women in a World at War: Contemporary Accounts from World War II*. Wilmington, Del.: Scholarly Resources, 1997.

Litoff, Judy Barrett, and David C. Smith, eds. *Since You Went Away: World War II Letters from American Women on the Home Front*. New York: Oxford University Press, 1991.

Madison, James H. *Slinging Doughnuts for the Boys: An American Woman in World War II*. Bloomington: Indiana University Press, 2007.

Parillo, Mark P. *We Were in the Big One: Experiences of the World War II Generation*. Wilmington, Del.: Scholarly Resources, 2002.

Stoler, Mark A., and Melanie S. Gustafson, eds. *Major Problems in the History of World War II: Documents and Essays*. Boston: Houghton Mifflin, 2003.

Takaki, Ronald. *Double Victory: A Multicultural History of America in World War II*. Boston: Little, Brown, 2000.

Terkel, Studs. *"The Good War": An Oral History of World War Two*. New York: Ballantine Books, 1984.

Uchida, Yoshiko. *Desert Exile: The Uprooting of a Japanese American Family*. Seattle: University of Washington Press, 1982.

Winkler, Allan M. *Home Front U.S.A.: America during World War II*. Second Edition. Wheeling, Ill.: Harlan Davidson, 2000.

Yellin, Emily. *Our Mothers' War: American Women at Home and at the Front during World War II*. New York: Free Press, 2004.

Military Experience

Ambrose, Stephen E. *Band of Brothers: E Company, 506th Regiment, 101st Airborne from Normandy to Hitler's Eagle's Nest*. New York: Simon & Shuster, 1992.

Atkinson, Rick. *An Army at Dawn: The War in North Africa, 1942–1943*. New York: Henry Holt, 2002.

Atkinson, Rick. *The Day of Battle: The War in Sicily and Italy, 1943–1944*. New York: Henry Holt, 2007.

Beevor, Antony. *The Fall of Berlin 1945*. New York: Viking, 2002.

Fussell, Paul. *Wartime: Understanding Behavior in the Second World War*. New York: Oxford University Press, 1989.

Hastings, Max. *Armageddon: The Battle for Germany 1944–1945*. New York: Vantage, 2004.

Hastings, Max. *Retribution: The Battle for Japan, 1944–1945*. New York: Random House, 2008.

Linderman, Gerald F. *The World within War: America's Combat Experience in World War II*. New York: Free Press, 1997.

Manchester, William. *Goodbye, Darkness: A Memoir of the Pacific War*. Boston: Little, Brown, 1979.

Mauldin, Bill. *Up Front*. New York: Henry Holt, 1945.

Pyle, Ernie. *Brave Men*. New York: Henry Holt, 1944.

Roberts, Geoffrey. *Victory at Stalingrad: The Battle That Changed History*. London: Longman, 2002.

Schrijvers, Peter. *The GI War against Japan: American Soldiers in Asia and the Pacific during World War II*. New York: New York University Press, 2002.

Sledge, E. B. *With the Old Breed: At Peleliu and Okinawa*. New York: Oxford University Press, 1981.

Everyday Life

Bird, William L., and Harry R. Rubenstein. *Design for Victory: World War II Posters on the American Home Front*. New York: Princeton Architectural Press, 1998.

Doherty, Thomas. *Projections of War: Hollywood, American Culture, and World War II*. New York: Columbia University Press, 1993.

Koppes, Clayton R., and Gregory D. Black. *Hollywood Goes to War: How Politics, Profits, and Propaganda Shaped World War II Movies*. Berkeley: University of California Press, 1987.

Minear, Richard H. *Dr. Seuss Goes to War: The World War II Editorial Cartoons of Theodor Seuss Geisel*. New York: New Press, 1999.

Paret, Peter, et al. *Persuasive Images: Posters of War and Revolution from the Hoover Institution Archives*. Princeton, N.J.: Princeton University Press, 1992.

Roeder, George H., Jr. *The Censored War: American Visual Experience during World War Two*. New Haven, Conn.: Yale University Press, 1993.

Werner, Emmy E., ed. *Through the Eyes of Innocents: Children Witness World War II*. Boulder, Colo.: Westview Press, 2000.

The Holocaust

Abzug, Robert H., ed. *America Views the Holocaust, 1933–1945: A Brief Documentary History*. Boston: Bedford/St. Martins, 1999.

Browning, Christopher R. *Ordinary Men: Reserve Police Battalion 101 and the Final Solution in Poland*. New York: HarperCollins, 1992.

Frank, Anne. *The Diary of a Young Girl*. New York: Bantam, 1997.

Gross, Jan T. *Neighbors: The Destruction of the Jewish Community in Jedwabne, Poland*. Princeton, N.J.: Princeton University Press, 2001.

Levi, Primo. *Survival in Auschwitz: The Nazi Assault on Humanity*. New York: Simon & Schuster, 1996.

Niewyk, Donald, and Francis Nicosia, eds. *The Columbia Guide to the Holocaust.* New York: Columbia University Press, 2000.

Spiegelman, Art. *Maus: A Survivor's Tale.* New York: Pantheon Books, 1986.

Wiesel, Eli. *Night.* New York: Hill and Wang, 1958.

Aftermath

Buruma, Ian. *Wages of Guilt: Memories of War in Germany and Japan.* New York: Meridian, 1994.

Dower, John W. *Embracing Defeat: Japan in the Wake of World War II.* New York: W.W. Norton, 1999.

Hersey, John. *Hiroshima.* New York: Knopf, 1946.

Judt, Tony. *Postwar: A History of Europe since 1945.* New York: Penguin, 2005.

Marrus, Michael R. *The Nuremberg War Crimes Trial, 1945–46.* Boston: Bedford Books, 1997.

Winkler, Allan M. *The Cold War: A History in Documents.* New York: Oxford University Press, 2003.

Websites

This list indicates a few of the more useful among the dozens of very good websites that offer primary sources on World War II. Many have links to other sites.

Australian War Memorial
http://www.awm.gov.au/index.asp

The museum provides a good introduction to Australia's role in the war.

Avalon Project at Yale Law School
http://avalon.law.yale.edu/subject_menus/wwii.asp

Full text of dozens of significant diplomatic and military documents of the war are available on this excellent site.

Canadian War Museum
http://www.warmuseum.ca/cwm/home/home

The museum focuses on how Canada's military past, including World War II, shaped the country.

Franklin D. Roosevelt Presidential Library
http://www.fdrlibrary.marist.edu/index.html

The wartime president's library has a very good selection of documents and photographs online, including audio clips of some of his speeches.

German Propaganda Archive
http://www.calvin.edu/academic/cas/gpa/ww2era.htm

Maintained at Calvin College in Michigan, this site provides English translations of dozens of Nazi articles, posters, and other propaganda.

Hiroshima Peace Memorial Museum
http://www.pcf.city.hiroshima.jp/index_e2.html

Located where the bomb fell, the museum's online exhibits show what happened to the people of the city.

Imperial War Museum
http://london.iwm.org.uk/server.php?show=nav.00b

This museum in London offers extensive online primary sources focused on Great Britain's role in the war, but extending to the British Empire.

Japanese American National Museum
http://www.janm.org

The museum explores the experience of Americans of Japanese ancestry, including internment during the war.

Le Mémorial de Caen
http://www.memorial-caen.fr/portail/index.php?lang=EN

Located in Normandy, this museum and its website focus on French experiences in the war and after.

Library of Congress
http://www.loc.gov/rr/program/bib/WW2/WW2bib.html

A guide to World War II sources on the numerous websites of the Library of Congress, including the Veterans History Project (http://www.memorial.fr/index.htm).

Museum of Tolerance
http://www.museumoftolerance.com/site/pp.asp?c=arLPK7PILqF&b=249627

This Los Angeles museum focuses on racism and the Holocaust.

Smithsonian National Museum of American History
http://americanhistory.si.edu/perfectunion/experience/index.html

"A More Perfect Union: Japanese Americans and the U.S. Constitution" is one of several good sites offered by the Smithsonian. This one provides interactive galleries of photographs, documents, and oral histories to study one of America's troubling legacies of the war.

Truman Presidential Museum and Library
http://www.trumanlibrary.org/index.html

A special section on President Truman and World War II includes many documents, posters, photographs, oral histories, and recordings.

United States Holocaust Memorial Museum
http://www.ushmm.org

Many online exhibitions and extensive sources make this museum in Washington, D.C., an essential point of study for the war's most difficult subject.

United States National Archives
http://www.archives.gov/research_room/research_topics/world_war_2_photos/world_war_2_photos.html#aid

The National Archives in Washington, D.C., has a large variety of online sources. This site provides a good selection of photographs, mostly military, grouped by subject matter.

United States National Archives
http://www.archives.gov/exhibits/powers_of_persuasion/powers_of_persuasion_home.html

A second National Archives site, "Powers of Persuasion," provides propaganda posters with very helpful descriptions and analyses of each.

Text Credits

Main Text

11: William L. Shirer, *Berlin Diary: The Journal of a Foreign Correspondent 1934–1941* (Boston: Little, Brown, 1941), 584, 586–87.

11–13: *Frauen-Warte* 22 (1936/37): 692–693, English translation at: www.calvin.edu/academic/cas/gpa/frau01.htm

13: Roderick Stackelberg and Sally A. Winkle, *The Nazi Germany Sourcebook: An Anthology of Texts* (London: Routledge, 2002), 190.

14–15: Richard Overy, *Interrogations: The Nazi Elite in Allied Hands, 1945* (New York: Viking, 2001), 332–33.

15: Dorothie Storry, *"Second Country": The Story of Richard Storry and Japan 1913–1982* (Woodchurch, England: Paul Norbury Publications, 1986), 41–43.

16: Timothy Brook, ed., *Documents on the Rape of Nanking* (Ann Arbor: University of Michigan Press, 1999), 214–15.

16–17: *New York Times*, August 22, 1939.

18: Avalon Project, Yale Law School, http://avalon.law.yale.edu/wwii/gb3.asp.

19–20: *Europe under the Nazi Scourge: A Picture & Indictment: A Reprint of Some Recent Articles in the* Times (London: Times Publishing, 1941), 36–37.

20–21: Fletcher Pratt, *Sea Power and Today's War* (New York: Harrison-Hilton Books, 1939), 177, 178–79, 180.

21: Judy Barrett Litoff and David C. Smith, eds., *Since You Went Away: World War II Letters from American Women on the Home Front* (New York: Oxford University Press, 1991), 9.

22–23: Roderick Stackelberg and Sally A. Winkle, eds., *The Nazi Germany Sourcebook: An Anthology of Texts* (London: Routledge, 2002), 290.

24: Roderick Stackelberg and Sally A. Winkle, eds., *The Nazi Germany Sourcebook: An Anthology of Texts* (London: Routledge, 2002), 291.

24–25: William L. Shirer, *Berlin Diary: The Journal of a Foreign Correspondent, 1934–1941* (Boston: Little, Brown, 1941), 419, 424–25.

25: Alex Danchev and Daniel Todman, eds., *War Diaries, 1939–1945: Field Marshal Lord Alanbrooke* (Berkeley: University of California Press, 2001), 105, 108.

26–27: UCLA Center for East Asian Studies, www.isop.ucla.edu/eas/documents/19420527-tojo.htm.

30: Department of the Navy, Naval Historical Center, www.history.navy.mil/faqs/faq60-10.htm.

30–31: Jon Guttman, "Tuskegee and Beyond," *Aviation History* 9 (March 1999): 41–42.

31–32: British Information Services, "Women's War Work in Britain" (November 1943): 8–9.

32: Anne Noggle, *A Dance with Death: Soviet Airwomen in World War II* (College Station: Texas A&M University Press, 1994), 39–40.

33: Ernie Pyle, *Here is Your War* (New York: Holt, Rinehart, & Winston, 1943), 222.

33–34: Omer Bartov, *The Eastern Front, 1941–45, German Troops and the Barbarisation of Warfare* (second edition, Basingstoke, England: Palgrave, 2001), 33.

34: Alexander Werth, *The Year of Stalingrad: A Historical Record and a Study of Russian Mentality, Methods, and Policies* (New York: Knopf, 1947), 341–42.

34–35: Haruko Taya Cook and Theodore F. Cook, eds., *Japan at War: An Oral History* (New York: New Press, 1992), 278.

35: William Manchester, *Goodbye Darkness: A Memoir of The Pacific War* (Boston, Little Brown, 1979), 257; Peter Schrijvers, *The GI War Against Japan: American Soldiers in Asia and the Pacific During World War II* (New York: New York University Press, 2002), 110.

35–36: Russell Cartwright Stroup, *Letters from the Pacific: A Combat Chaplain in World War II* (Columbia: University of Missouri Press, 2000), 158.

37: Michael E. Stevens and Ellen D. Goldlust, eds., *Women Remember the War, 1941–1945* (Madison: State Historical Society of Wisconsin, 1993), 130–31, 132; Charles E. (Commando) Kelly, *One Man's War* (New York, Alfred A. Knopf, 1944), 126.

37–38: James Tobin, *Ernie Pyle's War: America's Eyewitness to World War II* (New York: Free Press, 1997), 4.

38: Randall Jarrell, *Little Friend, Little Friend* (New York: Dial Press, 1945), 15–16.

38–39: Tamasin Day-Lewis, *Last Letters Home* (Basingstoke, England: Macmillan, 1995), 131.

39–41: Günter Grass, *Peeling the Onion* (New York: Harcourt, 2007), 123–125.

41: *Yank*, January 21, 1945.

42: Christopher R. Browning, *Ordinary Men: Reserve Police Battalion 101 and the Final Solution in Poland* (New York: HarperCollins, 1992), 138–39.

42–43: Haruko Taya Cook and Theodore F. Cook, eds., *Japan at War: An Oral History* (New York: New Press, 1992), 272.

43: E.B. Sledge, *With the Old Breed: At Peleliu and Okinawa* (New York: Oxford University Press, 1981, 1990), 120.

44–45: R. John Pritchard and Sonia Magbanua Zaide, eds., *The Tokyo War Crimes Trial*, vol. 3 (New York: Garland, 1981), 5471–5473.

48: Haruko Taya Cook and Theodore F. Cook, eds., *Japan at War: An Oral History* (New York: New Press, 1992), 138.

49: Franklin D. Roosevelt Presidential Library, www.fdrlibrary.marist.edu/120941.html.

49–50: Alexander Werth, *Russia At War 1941–1945* (New York: Carroll & Graf, 1964), 219.

50: Franklin D. Roosevelt Presidential Library, www.fdrlibrary.marist.edu/101242.html.

52: British Information Services, "Women's War Work in Britain" (November 1943): 2, 7–8.

52–53: Michael E. Stevens and Ellen D. Goldlust, eds., *Women Remember the War 1941–1945* (Madison: State Historical Society of Wisconsin, 1993), 12.

53–55: Primo Levi, *Survival in Auschwitz: The Nazi Assault on Humanity* (New York: Simon & Schuster, 1996), 25, 72–73.

55: Franklin D. Roosevelt Presidential Library, www.fdrlibrary.marist.edu/061244.html.

56: Richard Overy, *Interrogations: The Nazi Elite in Allied Hands, 1945* (New York: Viking, 2001), 349, 350.

56–57: Robert Easton and Jane Easton, *Love and War: Pearl Harbor Through V-J Day* (Norman, University of Oklahoma Press, 1991), 229.

60: Martin Gilbert, ed., *The Churchill War Papers, Volume II: Never Surrender, May 1940–December 1940* (New York: Norton, 1995), 22.

60–63: Joseph Stalin, *The Great Patriotic War of the Soviet Union* (New York: International Publishers, 1945), 9–17.

63: Ken'ichi Goto, *Tensions of Empire: Japan and Southeast Asia in the Colonial and Postcolonial World* (Athens: Ohio University Press, 2003), 39; Thomas Doherty, *Projections of War: Hollywood, American Culture, and World War II* (New York: Columbia University Press, 1993), 168.

63–64: Samuel I. Rosenman, ed., *The Public Papers and Addresses of Franklin D. Roosevelt: 1942; Humanity on the Defensive* (New York: Harper Brothers, 1950), 223.

64–65: *Newsweek*, March 22, 1943.

65: Michael E. Stevens and Ellen D. Goldlust, eds., *Women Remember the War 1941–1945* (Madison: State Historical Society of Wisconsin, 1993), 83, 84.

65–66: Mollie Panter-Downes, *London War Notes, 1939–1945* (New York: Farrar, Straus and Giroux, 1971), 160–63.

66–67: British Information Services, *The Production and Distribution of Food in Great Britain* (October 1943), 17.

67: David M. Glantz, *The Battle for Leningrad, 1941–1944* (Lawrence: University Press of Kansas, 2002), 136.

67–68: Franklin D. Roosevelt Presidential Library, www.fdrlibrary.marist.edu/072843.html.

68: *If Your Baby Must Travel in Wartime* (Washington, DC: Children's Bureau, US Department of Labor, 1944), 3.

69: Chang-Tai Hung, *War and Popular Culture: Resistance in Modern China, 1937–1945* (Berkley: University of California Press, 1994), 154.

70: "Notes on the Way," *Time and Tide,* October 5, 1940, quoted in Jenny Hartley, ed., *Hearts Undefeated: Women's Writing of the Second World War* (London: Virago, 1994), 93.

70–71: British Information Services, *Juvenile Delinquency in Britain during the War* (April 1944), 3–4.

71–72: Jeremy Noakes, ed., *Nazism 1919–1945, Volume 4: The German Home Front in World War II, A Documentary Reader* (Exeter: University of Exeter Press, 1998), 554, 556–57.

72–73: United States Strategic Bombing Survey, *Summary Report (Pacific War)* (Washington, D.C., 1946), 16, 17, 20.

73–74: Mark Stoler and Melanie S. Gustafson, eds., *Major Problems in the History of World War II* (Boston, 2003), 115. Permission from Hoover Institution Archives.

74: Roderick Stackelberg and Sally A. Winkle, *The Nazi Germany Sourcebook: An Anthology of Texts* (London, Routledge, 2002), 305–06.

75–77: Yoshiko Uchida, *Desert Exile: The Uprooting of a Japanese-American Family* (Seattle: University of Washington Press, 1982), 106, 109, 110.

77–78: Walter White, *A Rising Wind* (Garden City, N.Y.: Doubleday, Doran and Company, 1945), 123–24.

78–79: Franklin D. Roosevelt Presidential Library, www.fdrlibrary.marist.edu/Tmirhi53.html.

79–80: Calvin College, www.calvin.edu/academic/cas/gpa/ads.htm.

80: Philomena Goodman, *Women, Sexuality and War* (Basingstoke, England: Palgrave, 2002), 135; David Reynolds, *Rich Relations: The American Occupation of Britain, 1942–1945* (New York: Harper Collins, 1995), 218.

81: Jeremy Noakes, ed., *Nazism 1919–1945, Volume 4: The German Home Front in World War II, A Documentary Reader* (Exeter: University of Exeter Press, 1998), 452–53.

92: Geoffrey Roberts, *Victory at Stalingrad: The Battle that Changed History* (London: Longman, 2002), 203, 205, 206, 208.

92–93: Alexander Werth, *Russia at War, 1941–1945* (New York: Carroll & Graf, 1964), 562–63.

93–95: Calvin College, www.calvin.edu/academic/cas/gpa/goeb36.htm.

95–96: John Steinbeck, *Once There Was a War* (New York: Viking Press, 1958), 171–72.

96: Hans-Adolf Jacobsen and Arthur L. Smith, Jr., *World War II: Policy and Strategy, Selected Documents with Commentary* (Santa Barbara, CA: Clio Books, 1979), 259–60.

99: Howard H. Peckham and Shirley A. Snyder, eds., *Letters form Fighting Hoosiers* (Bloomington: Indiana War History Commission, 1948), 121–22.

100: Judy Barrett Litoff and David C. Smith, eds., *Since You Went Away: World War II Letters From American Women on the Home Front* (New York: Oxford University Press, 1991), 237.

101: Roderick Stackelberg and Sally A. Winkle, eds., *The Nazi Germany Sourcebook: An Anthology of Texts* (London: Routledge, 2002), 327.

101–104: Anthony Beevor and Luba Vinogradova, ed. and trans., *A Writer at War: Vasily Grossman with the Red Army 1941–1945* (New York, Pantheon Books, 2005), 338–339, 341–42.

104: Alexander Werth, *Russia at War, 1941–1945* (New York: Carroll & Graf, 1964), 986.

105: Roy E. Appleman, James M. Burns, Russell A. Gugeler, and John Stevens, *Okinawa: The Last Battle* (Washington, D.C.: United States Army, 1948), 489.

105–106: William Manchester, *Goodbye Darkness: A Memoir of the Pacific War* (Boston: Little, Brown, 1979), 373–374, 375, 384.

106–107: Harry S. Truman Presidential Library, www.trumanlibrary.org/whistlestop/study_collections/bomb/ferrell_book/ferrell_book_chap5.htm.

107–109: Harry S. Truman Presidential Library, http://trumanlibrary.org/publicpapers/index.php?pid=100&st=&st1.

109: Robert J. C. Butow, *Japan's Decision to Surrender* (Stanford: Stanford University Press, 1954), 248.

114: Judy Barrett Litoff and David C. Smith, eds., *Since You Went Away: World War II Letters From American Women on the Home Front* (New York: Oxford University Press, 1991), 269.

115: Michael E. Stevens and Ellen D. Goldlust, eds., *Women Remember the War, 1941–1945* (Madison: State Historical Society of Wisconsin, 1993), 138; Alex Danchev and Daniel Todman, eds., *War Diaries, 1939–1945: Field Marshal Lord Alan Brooke* (Berkeley: University of California Press, 2001), 718.

115–116: Harry S. Truman Presidential Library, www.trumanlibrary.org/publicpapers/index.php?pid=129&st=surrender&st1.

116: Ulrike Jordan, ed., *Conditions of Surrender: Britons and Germans Witness the End of the War* (London: I. B. Tauris, 1997), 89, 90.

117–118: Martha Gellhorn, *The Face of War* (New York: Simon and Schuster, 1959), 213–14.

118: Richard Overy, *Interrogations: the Nazi Elite in Allied Hands* (New York: Viking, 2001), 499.

119: Ulrike Jordan, ed., *Conditions of Surrender: Britons and Germans Witness the End of the War* (London: I. B. Tauris, 1997), 106–107.

119–121: *Nuremberg Trial Proceedings,* Vol. 6, http://avalon.law.yale.edu/imt/01-28-46.asp.

121–122: Timothy Brook, ed., *Documents on the Rape of Nanking* (Ann Arbor: University of Michigan Press, 1999), 266, 267.

122–123: Arthur Marwick and Wendy Simpson, eds., *War, Peace and Social Change: Documents 2: 1925–1959* (Buckingham, UK: Open University Press, 1990), 169–171.

123–124: Roderick Stackelberg and Sally A. Winkle, eds., *The Nazi Germany Sourcebook: An Anthology of Texts* (London: Routledge, 2002), 382, 384.

124: Haruko Taya Cook and Theodore F. Cook, eds., *Japan at War: An Oral History* (New York: New Press, 1992), 469; National Diet Library, www.ndl.go.jp/constitution/e/etc/c01.html#2.

125: National Diet Library, www.ndl.go.jp/constitution/e/etc/c01.html#3.

125–126: Karon S. Bailey, "Harriett Engelhardt: A Job Worth Having," *Alabama Heritage* (Summer 2000): 33.

126: Harry S. Truman Presidential Library, www.trumanlibrary.org/hoover/world.htm.

126–127: Franklin D. Roosevelt Presidential Library, www.fdrlibrary.marist.edu/odgist.html.

127–128: Amram Scheinfeld, "Motherhood's Back in Style," *Ladies' Home Journal* (September 19, 1944): 136, 159.

128: Records of the Women's Bureau, RG 86, National Archives, in *Documents from the National Archives: Women in Industry World War II* (Dubuque, Iowa: Kendall/Hunt, nd), 42–43.

129: *Services for Unmarried Mothers and Their Children* (Washington, DC: Children's Bureau, U.S. Department of Labor, 1945), 1–2.

130: Walter White, *A Rising Wind* (Garden City, N.Y.: Doubleday, Doran and Company, 1945), 142–44, 155.

131: The Universal Declaration of Human Rights, www.un.org/Overview/rights.html.

134: Judy Barrett Litoff and David C. Smith, *Since You Went Away: World II Letters from American Women on the Home Front* (New York: Oxford University Press, 1991), 276–77.

135: Studs Terkel, *"The Good War": An Oral History of World War Two* (New York: Ballantine Books, 1984), 108.

135–136: Anthony Beevor and Luba Vinogradova, ed. and trans., *A Writer at War: Vasily Grossman with the Red Army 1941–1945* (New York, Pantheon Books, 2005), 348.

136: J. L. Granatstein and Desmond Morton, *A Nation Forged in Fire: Canadians and the Second World War 1939–1945* (Toronto: Lester & Orpen Denny, 1989), 246–47.

136–137: Elie Wiesel, *Night* (New York: Hill and Wang, 1960), 43–44.

137: *New York Times,* October 19, 1988.

137–138: Maria Rosa Henson, *Comfort Woman: A Filipina's Story of Prostitution and Slavery under the Japanese Military* (Lanham, Md: Rowman & Littlefield Publishers, 1999), 36, 39.

138–139: Gerald R. Ford Library and Museum, http://www.ford.utexas.edu/library/speeches/760111p.htm.

140–141: John T. Correll, "War Stories at Air and Space," *Air Force Magazine* (April 1994), 24.

141: *Time,* January 4, 1971.

Sidebars

11: Quoted in Herbert P. Bix, *Hirohito and the Making of Modern Japan* (New York: Harper Collins, 2000), 374.

14: Entertonement, www.entertonement.com/clips/pgqhytsngz-Not-Interested-In-PoliticsCasablanca-Humphrey-Bogart-Rick-Blaine-.

18: Elizabeth Mullener, *War Stories: Remembering World War II* (Baton Rouge: Louisiana State University Press, 2002), 5.

21: Howard H. Peckham and Shirley A. Snyder, eds., *Letters form Fighting Hoosiers* (Bloomington: Indiana War History Commission, 1948), 9–10.

25: Martin Gilbert, ed., *The Churchill War Papers, Volume II: Never Surrender, May 1940–December 1940* (New York: Norton, 1995), 247.

32: F.T. Prince, *Collected Poems 1935–1992* (Manchester, England: Carcanet Press, 1993), 55.

33: James H. Madison, *Slinging Doughnuts for the Boys: An American Woman in World War II* (Bloomington: Indiana University Press), 111–12, 221.

34: Alexander Werth, *Russia at War 1941–1945* (New York: Carroll & Graff, 1964), 274.

36: "Don't Sit under the Apple Tree," Alfred Publishing Company, 1942.

37: Michael E. Stevens and Ellen D. Goldlust, eds., *Women Remember the War, 1941–1945* (Madison: State Historical Society of Wisconsin, 1993), 99.

42: Gerald F. Linderman, *The World Within War: America's Combat Experience in World War II* (New York: Free Press, 1997), 138.

43: Haruko Taya Cook and Theodore F. Cook, eds., *Japan at War: An Oral History* (New York: New Press, 1992), 289; Howard H. Peckham and Shirley A. Snyder, eds., *Letters form Fighting Hoosiers* (Bloomington: Indiana War History Commission, 1948), 244.

48: Richard Overy, *Why the Allies Won* (New York: Norton, 1995), 234.

50: John Barber and Mark Harrison, *The Soviet Home Front, 1941–1945: A Social and Economic History of the USSR in World War II* (London, Longman, 1991), 131.

51: Franklin D. Roosevelt Presidential Library. www.fdrlibrary.marist.edu/090742.html

52: Arthur Wauters, *Eve in Overalls* (Imperial War Museum reprint, 2001), 35.

53: Chad Berry, *Southern Migrants, Northern Exiles* (Urbana: University of Illinois Press, 2000), 96.

54: Thomas R. H. Havens, *Valley of Darkness: The Japanese People and World War Two* (New York: Norton, 1978), 109.

63: Studs Terkel, *"The Good War": An Oral History of World War Two* (New York: Ballantine Books, 1984), 243.

67: Franklin Delano Roosevelt Library, www.fdrlibrary.marist.edu/072843.html; Thomas R. H. Havens, *Valley of Darkness: The Japanese People and World War Two* (Lanham, M.D., 1986), 166.

68: John Bodnar, *Our Towns: Remembering Community in Indiana* (Indianapolis: Indiana Historical Society, 2001), 67.

69: *Persuading the People* (London: HMSO, 1995), 11.

73: Haruko Taya Cook and Theodore F. Cook, eds., *Japan at War: An Oral History* (New York: New Press, 1992), 337.

74: Thomas R. Searle, "It Made a Lot of Sense to Kill Skilled Workers": The Firebombing of Tokyo in March 1945," *Journal of Military History* 66 (January 2002): 118.

77: Sherna Berger Gluck, *Rosie the Riveter Revisited: Women, The War and Social Change* (New York, Meridian, 1988), 23.

80: Libby Connors, Lynette Finch, Kay Saunders, Helen Taylor, eds., *Australia's Frontline: Remembering the 1939–1945 War* (Queensland: University of Queensland Press, 1992), 146.

83: William L. Bird, Jr., and Harry R. Rubenstein, *Design for Victory: World War II Posters on the American Home Font* (New York: Princeton Architectural Press, 1998), 11.

92: Alexander Werth, *The Year of Stalingrad: A Historical Record and a Study of Russian Mentality, Methods, and Policies* (New York: Knopf, 1946), 172.

93: Robert Easton and Jane Easton, *Love and War: Pearl Harbor Through V-J Day* (Norman: University of Oklahoma Press, 1991), 4; Jeremy Noakes, ed., *Nazism 1919–1945, Volume 4: The German Home Front in World War II, A Documentary Reader* (Exeter: University of Exeter Press, 1998), 549.

98: Jeremy Noakes and G. Pridham, eds., *Nazism 1919–1945, Volume 2: Foreign Policy, War and Racial Extermination* (New York: Schocken Books, 1988), 870–71.

104: Anthony Beevor, *The Fall of Berlin* (New York: Viking, 2002), 190; Anonymous, *A Woman in Berlin; Eight weeks in the Conquered City: A Diary* (New York: Picador, 2006), 61.

105: E. B. Sledge, *With the Old Breed at Peleliu and Okinawa* (New York: Oxford University Press, 1981), 312.

106: Haruko Taya Cook and Theodore F. Cook, *Japan at War: An Oral History* (New York: New Press, 1992), 327.

109: Haruko Taya Cook and Theodore F. Cook, eds., *Japan at War: An Oral History* (New York: New Press, 1992), 280.

113: The Churchill Society, www.churchill-society-london.org.uk/YrVictry.html.

114: William M. Tuttle, Jr., *"Daddy's Gone to War": The Second World War in the Lives of America's Children* (New York: Oxford University Press, 1993), 215; *New York Times,* August 15, 1945.

115: Howard H. Peckham and Shirley A. Snyder, eds., *Letters form Fighting Hoosiers* (Bloomington: Indiana War History Commission, 1948), 220; Richard Overy, *Russia's War* (New York: Penguin Books, 1997), 255.

119: Bernard Rice, "Recollections of a World War II Combat Medic," *Indiana Magazine of History* (December 1997): 335.

121: Timothy Brook, ed., *Documents on the Rape of Nanking* (Ann Arbor: University of Michigan Press, 1999), 293, 294; John W. Dower, *Embracing Defeat: Japan in the Wake of World War II* (New York: W. W. Norton, 1999), 475.

124: John W. Dower, *Embracing Defeat: Japan in the Wake of World War II* (New York: W. W. Norton, 1999), 418.

125: Beate Sirota Gordon, *The Only Woman in the Room* (Tokyo: Kodansha International 1997), 108; John W. Dower, *Embracing Defeat: Japan in the Wake of World War II* (W.W. Norton, New York, 1999), 48.

126: Amy Bentley, *Eating for Victory: Food Rationing and the Politics of Domesticity* (Urbana: University of Illinois Press, 1998), 150.

134: Studs Terkel, *"The Good War": An Oral History of World War Two* (New York: Ballantine Books, 1984), 142; John Steinbeck, *Once There Was A War* (New York: Viking Press, 1958), xi.

135: E. B. Sledge, *With the Old Breed at Peleliu and Okinawa* (New York: Oxford University Press, 1981), xxi.

138: H. Res. 121, House of Representatives, U. S., July 30, 2007, http://frwebgate.access.gpo.gov/cgi-bin/getdoc.cgi?dbname=110_cong_bills&docid=f:hr121eh.txt.pdf.

140: *Atlanta Journal and Constitution,* June 23, 1994.

141: *New York Times,* May 12, 1985.

Picture Credits

Frontispiece: National Archives, Heinrich Hoffmann Collection, NWDNS-242-HLB-5073-20; Title page: National Archives, NWDNS-80-G-323712; vi: Collection of the Supreme Court of the United States; Library of Congress, LC-USZ62-50852; vii: National Archives, RG11; British Library, Cott. Vit. A XV f. 187 8152109; © Victoria and Albert Museum, London; ix: National Archives, NWDNS-208-PP-10A-3; Franklin Delano Roosevelt Library; x: Imperial War Museum, HU 36188; 4: National Archives, NWDNS-127-N-114541; 8: National Archives, NWDNS-242-EB-7(38); 10: Imperial War Museum, CH 740; 12: Library of Congress, LC-USZ62-115933; 13: Calvin College GPA; 15: Hoover Institution Archives Randall Chase Gould Collection, East Asia Vault, 2991.1-2314; 16: Courtesy of Daqing Yang; 19: Erich Lessing / Art Resource, NY; 20: National Archives, NWDNS-80-G-30549; 21: National Archives and Records Administration, General Records of the Department of the Navy, 1798-1947, NWDNS-80-G-16871; 22: Library of Congress, LC-USZ62-128756; Franklin Delano Roosevelt Library; 23: National Air and Space Museum, Smithsonian Institution (SI 91-13276); 25: National Archives, NWDNS-208-PP-10A-3l 26: Franklin Delano Roosevelt Library, 65386(36); 28: National Archives and Records Administration, General Records of the Department of the Navy, 1798-1947, NWDNS-80-G-468912; 30: The John F. Kennedy Presidential Library, Boston; 31: Imperial War Museum, H 14189l 33: National Archives, NWDNS-111-SC-198849; 35: Library of Congress, LC-USZ62-133012; 36: Calvin College GPA; 37: Courtesy of the Lilly Library, Indiana University, Bloomington, IN; 38: Australian War Memorial Negative Number ART26265; 39: National Archives, NWDNS-242-GAP-286B(4); 40: Library of Congress, LC-USZ62-48646; 41: Franklin Delano Roosevelt Library, Library ID 74596; 44: Australian War Memorial Negative Number 118879; 46: Franklin Delano Roosevelt Library, Library ID 66129(31); 48: Imperial War Museum, MH 4735; 49: National Archives, NWDNS-208-AA-352QQ(5) 51: Women of Canada Get Ready to Register, Hamilton Spectator collection, © Canadian War Museum; 52: Hoover Institution, Political Poster collection, Stanford University, RU/SU 2159; 53: Library of Congress, LC-USZC4-4442; 54: Auschwitz-Birkenau Museum and Memorial; 56: Hoover Institution, Political Poster collection, Stanford University, US 6035; 58: Library of Congress, LC-USZ62-94454; 60: Daily Express, June 1940; 61: Hoover Institution, Political Poster collection, Stanford University, RU/SU 2217; 64: Franklin Delano Roosevelt Library, Library ID 66158(6); 65: Franklin Delano Roosevelt Library, Library ID 7769(161); 66: Imperial War Museum D 24983; 68: Northwestern University Library; 69: Jianwen 1 (1 August 1938); 2; 70: Calvin College GPA; 71: Hoover Institution, Political Poster collection, Stanford University, GE1162; 72: National Archives 80-G-490421; 75: Franklin Delano Roosevelt Library, Library ID 65690(6); 76: Dr. Seuss Collection in the Mandeville Special Collections Library at the University of California, San Diego; 77: National Park Service, Abbie Rowe, Courtesy of Harry S. Truman Library; 78: Library of Congress, LC-USW3-026442-E; 79: Calvin College GPA; 81: Library of Congress, LC-USW3-023094-E; 82: Gordon Parks, photographer, Library of Congress, Prints & Photographs Division, LC-USW3-012129-C; 84: Library of Congress, LC-DIG-ppmsca-12900; Library of Congress LC-USZ62-76228; 85: Attack on All Fronts, 19730004-030 © Canadian War Museum; The Spirit of Canada's Women, 19750251-008 © Canadian War Museum; 86: NARA Still Picture Branch (NWDNS-179-WP01563); Imperial War Museum, IWM PST 2832; 87: NARA Still Picture Branch (NWDNS-44-PA-97); Ohio Historical Society; 88: Library of Congress LC-USZC2-109; Bundesarchiv Plak 003-023-089; Hoover Institution, Political Poster collection, Stanford University, US 6242; 89: Hoover Institution, Political Poster collection, Stanford University, US JA 59; NARA Still Picture Branch (NWDNS-208-PMP-68); Hoover Institution, Political Poster collection, Stanford University, RU/SU 2169; 90: National Archives, NWDNS-80-G-323712; 92: Imperial War Museum HU 5131; 94: Granger Collection, New York; 95: Library of Congress, LC-USZ62-84161; 96: U.S. Army photograph, Library of Congress, USZ62-25600; 97: Eisenhower Library; 98: Eisenhower Library; 99: National Archives and Records Administration, Records fo the U.S. Coast Guard, NWDNS-26-G-2343; 100: Library of Congress, LC-USZ62-90256; 102: Library of Congress, LC-USZ62-62165; National Archives, NWDNS-80-GK-5645; 103: National Archives NWDNS-208-YE-122; 107: National Archives, NWDNS-80-G-413988; 108: National Archives, NWDNS-208-N-43888; 110: Papers of Harry S. Truman, WHCF: Official File, OF 692-A; 111: Papers of Harry S. Truman, WHCF: Official File, OF 692-A; 112: Imperial War Museum H 41849; 114: National Archives, NWDNS-80-G-377094, War and Conflict Number 1358; 116: National Archives and Records Administration, Records of the Office of the Chief Signal Officer, NWDNS-111-SC-206406; 117: Eisenhower Library; 118: Eisenhower Library, 68-509-1; 119: United States Holocaust Memorial Museum, Photograph #89153; 120: United States Holocaust Memorial Museum, Photograph #81989; 122: Imperial War Museum, HU 69972; 123: Library of Congress, LC-USZ62-111645; 125: Library of Congress, LC-USZ62-134142; 127: © Washington Post. Reprinted by permission of the Washington, D.C., Public Library; 130: Southern Labor Archives, Georgia State University, Accession Number: L1979-34_10; 132: American Battle Monuments Commission; 135: AP Images / Mikhail Metzel; 136: United States Holocaust Memorial Museum, Photograph #74607; 137: Imperial War Museum, SE 4523; 138: Seabrook Educational and Cultural Center; 140: Smithsonian National Air and Space Museum; 141: © Hiromi Tsuchida

Acknowledgments

I am grateful to the librarians, scholars, museum curators, and many others who have done so much to preserve, understand, and share the history of World War II. I am especially grateful to the librarians at Indiana University whose good work was essential to preparing this book. Sarah Deutsch, Robert Moeller, and Jeffrey Wasserstrom, editors of the Pages from History series, made substantial improvements on an early draft. Several anonymous readers helped me rethink sections of the manuscript. Nancy Toff at Oxford University Press has provided expert advice and help from the beginning. I'm grateful also to Karen S. Fein, Lisa Grzan, Paula Schlosser, and Sonia Tycko, who expertly moved the manuscript to a book. Colleagues and students at Indiana University have been essential to my continued learning.

Index

Page numbers in **bold** indicate illustrations.

About the Author

James H. Madison is the Thomas and Kathryn Miller Professor of History and former chair of the Department of History, Indiana University, Bloomington. He is a Distinguished Teaching Award winner at the university, where he teaches classes on World War II and twentieth-century United States history. He has also taught, as a Fulbright Professor, at Hiroshima University, Japan, and at the University of Kent, Canterbury, England. His most recent books are *A Lynching in the Heartland: Race and Memory in America* and *Slinging Doughnuts for the Boys: An American Woman in World War II.*